PLAYS

BY

JOHN GALSWORTHY

PLAYS:

THE SILVER BOX
JOY
STRIFE

BY

JOHN GALSWORTHY

LONDON
DUCKWORTH AND CO.
HENRIETTA ST. COVENT GARDEN
1909

TO

H. GRANVILLE BARKER

CONTENTS

THE SILVER BOX

A COMEDY IN THREE ACTS

A

PERSONS OF THE PLAY

JOHN BARTHWICK, M.P., *a wealthy Liberal*
MRS. BARTHWICK, *his wife*
JACK BARTHWICK, *their son*
ROPER, *their solicitor*
MRS. JONES, *their charwoman*
MARLOW, *their manservant*
WHEELER, *their maidservant*
JONES, *the stranger within their gates*
MRS. SEDDON, *a landlady*
SNOW, *a detective*
A POLICE MAGISTRATE
AN UNKNOWN LADY, *from beyond*
TWO LITTLE GIRLS, *homeless*
LIVENS, *their father*
A RELIEVING OFFICER
A MAGISTRATE'S CLERK
AN USHER
POLICEMEN, CLERKS, AND OTHERS

TIME · The present. The action of the first two Acts takes place on Easter Tuesday ; the action of the third on Easter Wednesday week.

ACT I., SCENE I. Rockingham Gate. John Barthwick's dining-room.

    SCENE II. The same.

    SCENE III. The same.

ACT II., SCENE I. The Jones' lodgings, Merthyr Street.

    SCENE II. John Barthwick's dining-room.

ACT III. A London police court.

CAST OF THE ORIGINAL PRODUCTION AT THE ROYAL COURT THEATRE, LONDON, ON SEPTEMBER 25, 1906

JOHN BARTHWICK, M.P.	*Mr. James Hearn*
MRS. BARTHWICK	*Miss Frances Ivor*
JACK BARTHWICK	*Mr. A. E. Matthews*
ROPER	*Mr. A. Goodsall*
MRS. JONES	*Miss Irene Rooke*
MARLOW	*Mr. Frederick Lloyd*
WHEELER	*Miss Gertrude Henriques*
JONES	*Mr. Norman McKinnell*
MRS. SEDDON	*Mrs. Charles Maltby*
SNOW	*Mr. Trevor Lowe*
A POLICE MAGISTRATE	*Mr. Athol Forde*
AN UNKNOWN LADY	*Miss Sydney Fairbrother*
LIVENS	*Mr. Edmund Gurney*
RELIEVING OFFICER	*Mr. Edmund Gwenn*
MAGISTRATE'S CLERK	*Mr. Lewis Casson*
USHER	*Mr. Norman Page*

ACT I

SCENE I

The curtain rises on the BARTHWICKS' *dining-room, large, modern, and well furnished ; the window curtains drawn. Electric light is burning. On the large round dining-table is set out a tray with whisky, a syphon, and a silver cigarette-box. It is past midnight.*

A fumbling is heard outside the door. It is opened suddenly ; JACK BARTHWICK *seems to fall into the room. He stands holding by the door knob, staring before him, with a beatific smile. He is in evening dress and opera hat, and carries in his hand a sky-blue velvet lady's reticule. His boyish face is freshly coloured and clean-shaven. An overcoat is hanging on his arm.*

JACK. Hello ! I've got home all ri—— [*Defiantly.*] Who says I sh'd never've opened th' door without 'sistance. [*He staggers in, fumbling with the reticule. A lady's handkerchief and purse of crimson silk fall out.*] Serve her joll' well right—everything droppin' out. Th' cat. I've scored her off—I've got her bag. [*He swings the reticule.*] Serves her joll' well right. [*He*

5

takes a cigarette out of the silver box and puts it in his mouth.]   Never gave tha' fellow anything ! [*He hunts through all his pockets and pulls a shilling out; it drops and rolls away. He looks for it.*]   Beastly shilling ! [*He looks again.*]   Base ingratitude!   Absolutely nothing. [*He laughs.*]   Mus' tell him I've got absolutely nothing.

> [*He lurches through the door and down a corridor, and presently returns, followed by* JONES, *who is advanced in liquor. *JONES, *about thirty years of age, has hollow cheeks, black circles round his eyes, and rusty clothes. He looks as though he might be unemployed, and enters in a hang-dog manner.*]

JACK. Sh ! sh ! sh ! Don't you make a noise, whatever you do. Shu' the door, an' have a drink. [*Very solemnly.*]   You helped me to open the door —I've got nothin' for you. This is my house. My father's name's Barthwick; he's Member of Parliament—Liberal Member of Parliament : I've told you that before. Have a drink ! [*He pours out whisky and drinks it up.*]   I'm not drunk—— [*Subsiding on a sofa.*] Tha's all right. Wha's your name ? My name's Barthwick, so's my father's; *I'm* a Liberal too—wha're you ?

JONES. [*In a thick, sardonic voice.*] I'm a bloomin' Conserv*ative*. My name's Jones ! My wife works 'ere; she's the char; she works 'ere.

JACK. Jones? [*He laughs.*]   There's 'nother Jones at college with me. I'm not a Socialist myself; I'm

a Liberal—there's ve-lill difference, because of the
principles of the Lib—Liberal Party.   We're all
equal before the law—tha's rot, tha's silly. [*Laughs.*]
Wha' was I about to say?   Give me some whisky.

> [JONES *gives him the whisky he desires, together
> with a squirt of syphon.*]

Wha' I was goin' tell you was—I've had a row with
her. [*He waves the reticule.*]   Have a drink, Jones—
sh'd never have got in without you—tha's why I'm
giving you a drink.   Don' care who knows I've scored
her off.   Th' cat! [*He throws his feet up on the sofa.*]
Don' you make a noise, whatever you do.   You pour
out a drink—you make yourself good long, long drink
—you take cigarette—you take anything you like.
Sh'd never have got in without you. [*Closing his
eyes.*]   You're a Tory—you're a Tory Socialist.   I'm
Liberal myself—have a drink—I'm an excel'nt chap.

> [*His head drops back.   He, smiling, falls asleep,
> and* JONES *stands looking at him; then,
> snatching up* JACK'S *glass, he drinks it off.
> He picks the reticule from off* JACK'S *shirt-
> front, holds it to the light, and smells at it.*]

JONES. Been on the tiles and brought 'ome some
of yer cat's fur. [*He stuffs it into* JACK'S *breast pocket.*]
JACK. [*Murmuring.*] I've scored you off!   You cat!

> [JONES *looks around him furtively; he pours
> out whisky and drinks it.   From the silver
> box he takes a cigarette, puffs at it, and drinks
> more whisky.   There is no sobriety left in
> him.*]

JONES. Fat lot o' things they've got 'ere ! [*He sees the crimson purse lying on the floor.*] More cats' fur. Puss, puss ! [*He fingers it, drops it on the tray, and looks at* JACK.] Calf ! Fat calf ! [*He sees his own presentment in a mirror. Lifting his hands, with fingers spread, he stares at it ; then looks again at* JACK, *clenching his fist as if to batter in his sleeping, smiling face. Suddenly he tilts the rest of the whisky into the glass and drinks it. With cunning glee he takes the silver box and purse and pockets them.*] I'll score *you* off too, that's wot I'll do !

[*He gives a little snarling laugh and lurches to the door. His shoulder rubs against the switch ; the light goes out. There is a sound as of a closing outer door.*

The curtain falls.

The curtain rises again at once.

SCENE II

In the BARTHWICKS' *dining-room.* JACK *is still asleep; the morning light is coming through the curtains. The time is half-past eight.* WHEELER, *brisk person, enters with a dust-pan, and* MRS. JONES *more slowly with a scuttle.*

WHEELER. [*Drawing the curtains.*] That precious husband of yours was round for you after you'd gone yesterday, Mrs. Jones. Wanted your money for drink, I suppose. He hangs about the corner here half the time. I saw him outside the "Goat and Bells" when I went to the post last night. If I were you I wouldn't live with him. I wouldn't live with a man that raised his hand to me. I wouldn't put up with it. Why don't you take the children and leave him? If you put up with 'im it'll only make him worse. I never can see why, because a man's married you, he should knock you about.

MRS. JONES. [*Slim, dark-eyed, and dark-haired; oval-faced, and with a smooth, soft, even voice; her manner patient, her way of talking quite impersonal; she wears a blue linen dress, and boots with holes.*] It was nearly two last night before he come home, and he wasn't himself. He made me get up, and he knocked me about; he didn't seem to know *what* he was saying or doing. Of course I *would* leave him, but I'm really afraid of what he'd do to me. He's such a violent man when he's not himself.

WHEELER. Why don't you get him locked up? You'll never have any peace until you get him locked up. If I were you I'd go to the police court to-morrow. That's what I would do.

MRS. JONES. Of course I ought to go, because he does treat me so badly when he's not himself. But you see, Bettina, he has a very hard time—he's been out of work two months, and it preys upon his mind. When he's in work he behaves himself much better. It's when he's out of work that he's so violent.

WHEELER. Well, if you won't take any steps you'll never get rid of him.

Mrs. Jones. Of course it's very wearing to me; I don't get my sleep at nights. And it's not as if I were getting help from him, because I have to do for the children and all of us. And he throws such dreadful things up at me, talks of my having men to follow me about. Such a thing never happens; no man ever speaks to me. And of course it's just the other way. It's what he does that's wrong and makes me so unhappy. And then he's always threatenin' to cut my throat if I leave him. It's all the drink, and things preying on his mind; he's not a bad man really. Sometimes he'll speak quite kind to me, but I've stood so much from him, I don't feel it in me to speak kind back, but just keep myself to myself. And he's all right with the children too, except when he's not himself.

Wheeler. You mean when he's drunk, the beauty.

Mrs. Jones. Yes. [*Without change of voice.*] There's the young gentleman asleep on the sofa.

[*They both look silently at Jack.*

Mrs. Jones. [*At last, in her soft voice.*] He doesn't look quite himself.

Wheeler. He's a young limb, that's what he is. It's my belief he was tipsy last night, like your husband. It's another kind of bein' out of work that sets *him* to drink. I'll go and tell Marlow. This is his job. [*She goes.*

[*Mrs. Jones, upon her knees, begins a gentle sweeping.*

Jack. [*Waking.*] Who's there? What is it?

MRS. JONES. It's me, sir, Mrs. Jones.

JACK. [*Sitting up and looking round.*] Where is it—what—what time is it?

MRS. JONES. It's getting on for nine o'clock, sir.

JACK. For nine! Why—what! [*Rising, and loosening his tongue; putting hand to his head, and staring hard at Mrs. Jones.*] Look here, you, Mrs.—Mrs. Jones—don't you say you caught me asleep here.

MRS. JONES. No, sir, of course I won't, sir.

JACK. It's quite an accident; I don't know how it happened. I must have forgotten to go to bed. It's a queer thing. I've got a most beastly headache. Mind you don't say anything, Mrs. Jones.

> [*Goes out and passes* MARLOW *in the doorway.* MARLOW *is young and quiet; he is clean-shaven, and his hair is brushed high from his forehead in a coxcomb. Incidentally a butler, he is first a man. He looks at* MRS. JONES, *and smiles a private smile.*

MARLOW. Not the first time, and won't be the last. Looked a bit dicky, eh, Mrs. Jones?

MRS. JONES. He didn't look quite himself. Of course I didn't take notice.

MARLOW. You're used to them. How's your old man?

MRS. JONES. [*Softly as throughout.*] Well, he was very bad last night; he didn't seem to know what he was about. He was very late, and he was most abusive. But now, of course, he's asleep.

MARLOW. That's his way of finding a job, eh?

MRS. JONES. As a rule, Mr. Marlow, he goes out

early every morning looking for work, and sometimes he comes in fit to drop—and of course I can't say he doesn't try to get it, because he does. Trade's very bad. [*She stands quite still, her pan and brush before her, at the beginning and the end of long vistas of experience, traversing them with her impersonal eye.*] But he's not a good husband to me—last night he hit me, and he was so dreadfully abusive.

MARLOW. Bank 'oliday, eh! He's too fond of the "Goat and Bells," that's what's the matter with him. I see him at the corner late every night. He hangs about.

MRS. JONES. He gets to feeling very low walking about all day after work, and being refused so often, and then when he gets a drop in him it goes to his head. But he shouldn't treat his wife as he treats me. Sometimes I've had to go and walk about at night, when he wouldn't let me stay in the room; but he's sorry for it afterwards. And he hangs about after me, he waits for me in the street; and I don't think he ought to, because I've always been a good wife to him. And I tell him Mrs. Barthwick wouldn't like him coming about the place. But that only makes him angry, and he says dreadful things about the gentry. Of course it was through me that he first lost his place, through his not treating me right; and that's made him bitter against the gentry. He had a very good place as groom in the country; but it made such a stir, because of course he didn't treat me right.

MARLOW. Got the sack?

MRS. JONES. Yes; his employer said he couldn't keep him, because there was a great deal of talk; and he said it was such a bad example. But it's very important for me to keep my work here; I have the three children, and I don't want him to come about after me in the streets, and make a disturbance as he sometimes does.

MARLOW. [*Holding up the empty decanter.*] Not a drain! Next time he hits you get a witness and go down to the court——

MRS. JONES. Yes, I think I've made up my mind. I think I ought to.

MARLOW. That's right. Where's the ciga——?

> [*He searches for the silver box; he looks at* MRS. JONES, *who is sweeping on her hands and knees; he checks himself and stands reflecting. From the tray he picks two half-smoked cigarettes, and reads the name on them.*

Nestor—where the deuce——?

> [*With a meditative air he looks again at* MRS. JONES, *and, taking up* JACK'S *overcoat, he searches in the pockets.* WHEELER, *with a tray of breakfast things, comes in.*

MARLOW. [*Aside to* WHEELER.] Have you seen the cigarette-box?

WHEELER. No.

MARLOW. Well, it's gone. I put it on the tray last night. And he's been smoking. [*Showing her the ends of cigarette.*] It's not in these pockets.   He can't have taken it upstairs this morning!   Have a good look in his room when he comes down.   Who's been in here?

WHEELER. Only me and Mrs. Jones.

MRS. JONES. I've finished here; shall I do the drawing-room now?

WHEELER. [*Looking at her doubtfully.*] Have you seen—— Better do the boudwower first.

      [MRS. JONES *goes out with pan and brush.*
        MARLOW *and* WHEELER *look each other in
        the face.*

MARLOW. It'll turn up.

WHEELER. [*Hesitating.*] You don't think *she*——
[*Nodding at the door.*]

MARLOW. [*Stoutly.*] I don't—I never believes anything of anybody.

WHEELER. But the master'll have to be told.

MARLOW. You wait a bit, and see if it don't turn up.   Suspicion's no business of ours.   I set my mind against it.

The curtain falls.

The curtain rises again at once.

SCENE III

BARTHWICK *and* MRS. BARTHWICK *are seated at the breakfast table.   He is a man between fifty and sixty;
quietly important, with a bald forehead, and pince-
nez, and the " Times" in his hand.   She is a lady of
nearly fifty, well dressed, with greyish hair, good fea-
tures, and a decided manner.   They face each other.*

BARTHWICK. [*From behind his paper.*] The Labour
man has got in at the by-election for Barnside, my
dear.

MRS. BARTHWICK. Another Labour ?   I can't think
what on earth the country is about.

BARTHWICK. I predicted it.   It's not a matter of
vast importance.

MRS. BARTHWICK. Not ?   How can you take it so
calmly, John ?   To me it's simply outrageous.   And
there you sit, you Liberals, and pretend to encourage
these people !

BARTHWICK. [*Frowning.*] The representation of all
parties is necessary for any proper reform, for any
proper social policy.

MRS. BARTHWICK. I've no patience with your talk of
reform—all that nonsense about social policy.   We
know perfectly well what it is they want ; they want
things for themselves.   Those Socialists and Labour
men are an absolutely selfish set of people.   They
have no sense of patriotism, like the upper classes ;
they simply want what we've got.

BARTHWICK. Want what we've got! [*He stares into space.*] My dear, what are you talking about ? [*With a contortion.*] I'm no alarmist.

MRS. BARTHWICK. Cream ? Quite uneducated men ! Wait until they begin to tax our investments. I'm convinced that when they once get a chance they will tax everything—they've no feeling for the country. You Liberals and Conservatives, you're all alike ; you don't see an inch before your noses. You've no imagination, not a scrap of imagination between you. You ought to join hands and nip it in the bud.

BARTHWICK. You're talking nonsense ! How is it possible for Liberals and Conservatives to join hands, as you call it ? That shows how absurd it is for women—— Why, the very essence of a Liberal is to trust in the people !

MRS. BARTHWICK. Now, John, eat your breakfast. As if there were any real difference between you and the Conservatives. All the upper classes have the same interests to protect, and the same principles. [*Calmly.*] Oh ! you're sitting upon a volcano, John.

BARTHWICK. What !

MRS. BARTHWICK. I read a letter in the paper yesterday. I forget the man's name, but it made the whole thing perfectly clear. You don't look things in the face.

BARTHWICK. Indeed ! [*Heavily.*] I am a Liberal ! Drop the subject, please !

MRS. BARTHWICK. Toast ? I quite agree with what this man says : Education is simply ruining the lower

classes. It unsettles them, and that's the worst thing
for us all. I see an enormous difference in the manner
of servants.

BARTHWICK. [*With suspicious emphasis.*] I welcome
any change that will lead to something better. [*He
opens a letter.*] H'm! This is that affair of Master
Jack's again. " High Street, Oxford. Sir, We have
received Mr. John Barthwick, Senior's, draft for forty
pounds." Oh! the letter's to him ! " We now en-
close the cheque you cashed with us, which, as we
stated in our previous letter, was not met on pre-
sentation at your bank. We are, Sir, yours obediently,
Moss and Sons, Tailors." H'm! [*Staring at the
cheque.*] A pretty business altogether! The boy
might have been prosecuted.

MRS. BARTHWICK. Come, John, you know Jack
didn't mean anything ; he only thought he was over-
drawing. I still think his bank ought to have cashed
that cheque. They must know your position.

BARTHWICK. [*Replacing in the envelope the letter and
the cheque.*] Much good that would have done him
in a court of law. [*He stops as* JACK *comes in, fasten-
ing his waistcoat and staunching a razor cut upon his
chin.*]

JACK. [*Sitting down between them, and speaking with
an artificial joviality.*] Sorry I'm late. [*He looks
lugubriously at the dishes.*] Tea, please, mother. Any
letters for me ? [BARTHWICK *hands the letter to him.*]
But look here, I say, this has been opened ! I do
wish you wouldn't——

B

BARTHWICK. [*Touching the envelope.*] I suppose I'm entitled to this name.

JACK. [*Sulkily.*] Well, I can't help having your name, father! [*He reads the letter, and mutters.*] Brutes!

BARTHWICK. [*Eyeing him.*] You don't deserve to be so well out of that.

JACK. Haven't you ragged me enough, dad?

MRS. BARTHWICK. Yes, John, let Jack have his breakfast.

BARTHWICK. If you hadn't had me to come to, where would you have been? It's the merest accident—suppose you had been the son of a poor man or a clerk. Obtaining money with a cheque you knew your bank could not meet. It might have ruined you for life. I can't see what's to become of you if these are your principles. I never did anything of the sort myself.

JACK. I expect you always had lots of money. If you've got plenty of money, of course——

BARTHWICK. On the contrary, I had not your advantages. My father kept me very short of money.

JACK. How much had you, dad?

BARTHWICK. It's not material. The question is, do you feel the gravity of what you did?

JACK. I don't know about the gravity. Of course, I'm very sorry if you think it was wrong. Haven't I said so! I should never have done it at all if I hadn't been so jolly hard up.

BARTHWICK. How much of that forty pounds have you got left, Jack?

JACK. [*Hesitating.*] I don't know—not much.

BARTHWICK. How much?

JACK. [*Desperately.*] I haven't got any.

BARTHWICK. What?

JACK. I know I've got the most beastly headache.
                    [*He leans his head on his hand.*

MRS. BARTHWICK. Headache? My dear boy! Can't you eat any breakfast?

JACK. [*Drawing in his breath.*] Too jolly bad!

MRS. BARTHWICK. I'm so sorry. Come with me dear; I'll give you something that will take it away at once.

> [*They leave the room; and* BARTHWICK, *tearing up the letter, goes to the fireplace and puts the pieces in the fire. While he is doing this* MARLOW *comes in, and, looking round him, is about quietly to withdraw.*

BARTHWICK. What's that? What d'you want?

MARLOW. I was looking for Mr. John, sir.

BARTHWICK. What d'you want Mr. John for?

MARLOW. [*With hesitation.*] I thought I should find him here, sir.

BARTHWICK. [*Suspiciously.*] Yes, but what do you want him for?

MARLOW. [*Offhandedly.*] There's a lady called—asked to speak to him for a minute, sir.

BARTHWICK. A lady, at this time in the morning. What sort of a lady?

MARLOW. [*Without expression in his voice.*] I can't tell, sir; no particular sort. She might be after

charity. She might be a Sister of Mercy, I should
think, sir.

BARTHWICK. Is she dressed like one ?

MARLOW. No, sir, she's in plain clothes, sir.

BARTHWICK. Didn't she say what she wanted ?

MARLOW. No, sir.

BARTHWICK. Where did you leave her ?

MARLOW. In the hall, sir.

BARTHWICK. In the hall ?   How do you know she's
not a thief—not got designs on the house?

MARLOW. No, sir, I don't fancy so, sir.

BARTHWICK. Well, show her in here ; I'll see her
myself.

> [MARLOW *goes out with a private gesture of dis-
> may.   He soon returns, ushering in a young
> pale lady with dark eyes and pretty figure, in
> a modish, black, but rather shabby dress, a
> black and white trimmed hat with a bunch of
> Parma violets wrongly placed, and fuzzy-
> spotted veil.   At the sight of* MR. BARTHWICK
> *she exhibits every sign of nervousness.* MAR-
> LOW *goes out.*

UNKNOWN LADY. Oh ! but—I beg pardon—there's
some mistake— I——   [*She turns to fly.*]

BARTHWICK. Whom did you want to see, madam ?

UNKNOWN. [*Stopping and looking back.*] It was Mr.
John Barthwick I wanted to see.

BARTHWICK. I am John Barthwick, madam. What
can I have the pleasure of doing for you ?

UNKNOWN. Oh ! I—I don't——   [*She drops her*

eyes. BARTHWICK *scrutinises her, and purses his lips.*]

BARTHWICK. It was my son, perhaps, you wished to see ?

UNKNOWN. [*Quickly.*] Yes, of course, it's your son.

BARTHWICK. May I ask whom I have the pleasure of speaking to ?

UNKNOWN. [*Appeal and hardiness upon her face.*] My name is—oh ! it doesn't matter—I don't want to make any fuss. I just want to see your son for a minute. [*Boldly.*] In fact, I *must* see him.

BARTHWICK. [*Controlling his uneasiness.*] My son is not very well. If necessary, no doubt I could attend to the matter ; be so kind as to let me know——

UNKNOWN. Oh ! but I *must* see him—I've come on purpose——[*She bursts out nervously.*] I don't want to make any fuss, but the fact is, last—last night your son took away—he took away my—— [*She stops.*]

BARTHWICK. [*Severely.*] Yes, madam, what ?

UNKNOWN. He took away my—my reticule.

BARTHWICK. Your reti——?

UNKNOWN. I don't care about the reticule ; it's not *that* I want—I'm sure I don't want to make any fuss—[*her face is quivering*]—but—but—all my money was in it !

BARTHWICK. In what—in what ?

UNKNOWN. In my purse, in the reticule. It was a crimson silk purse. Really, I wouldn't have come—I don't want to make any fuss. But I must get my money back—mustn't I ?

BARTHWICK. Do you tell me that my son—— ?

UNKNOWN. Oh! well, you see, he wasn't quite—I mean he was——   [*She smiles mesmerically.*

BARTHWICK. I beg your pardon.

UNKNOWN. [*Stamping her foot.*] Oh! don't you see—tipsy! We had a quarrel.

BARTHWICK. [*Scandalised.*] How? Where?

UNKNOWN. [*Defiantly.*] At my place. We'd had supper at the——and your son——

BARTHWICK. [*Pressing the bell.*] May I ask how you knew this house? Did he give you his name and address?

UNKNOWN. [*Glancing sidelong.*] I got it out of his overcoat.

BARTHWICK. [*Sardonically.*] Oh! you got it out of his overcoat. And may I ask if my son will know you by daylight?

UNKNOWN. Know me? I should jolly—I mean, of course he will!   [MARLOW *comes in.*

BARTHWICK. Ask Mr. John to come down.

> [MARLOW *goes out, and* BARTHWICK *walks uneasily about.*

And how long have you enjoyed his acquaintanceship?

UNKNOWN. Only since—only since Good Friday.

BARTHWICK. I am at a loss—I repeat I am at a loss——

> [*He glances at this unknown lady, who stands with eyes cast down, twisting her hands. And suddenly Jack appears. He stops on seeing*

> *who is here, and the unknown lady hys-*
> *terically giggles. There is a silence.*

BARTHWICK. [*Portentously.*] This young—er—lady says that last night—I think you said last night, madam—you took away——

UNKNOWN. [*Impulsively.*] My reticule, and all my money was in a crimson silk purse.

JACK. Reticule. [*Looking round for any chance to get away.*] I don't know anything about it.

BARTHWICK. [*Sharply.*] Come, do you deny seeing this young lady last night?

JACK. Deny? No, of course. [*Whispering.*] Why did you give me away like this? What on earth did you come here for?

UNKNOWN. [*Tearfully.*] I'm sure I didn't want to—it's not likely, is it? You snatched it out of my hand—you know you did—and the purse had all my money in it. I didn't follow you last night because I didn't want to make a fuss and it was so late, and you were so——

BARTHWICK. Come, sir, don't turn your back on me—explain!

JACK. [*Desperately.*] I don't remember anything about it. [*In a low voice to his friend.*] Why on earth couldn't you have written?

UNKNOWN. [*Sullenly.*] I want it now; I must have it—I've got to pay my rent to-day. [*She looks at* BARTHWICK.] They're only too glad to jump on people who are not—not *well off*.

JACK. I don't remember anything about it, really. I don't remember anything about last night at all.

[*He puts his hand up to his head.*] It's all—cloudy, and I've got such a beastly headache.

UNKNOWN. But you *took* it; you know you did. You said you'd score me off.

JACK. Well, then, it must be here. I remember now—I remember something. Why did I take the beastly thing?

BARTHWICK. Yes, why did you take the beastly——
                     [*He turns abruptly to the window.*

UNKNOWN. [*With her mesmeric smile.*] You weren't quite——were you?

JACK. [*Smiling pallidly.*] I'm *awfully* sorry. If there's anything I can do——

BARTHWICK. Do? You can restore this property, I suppose.

JACK. I'll go and have a look, but I really don't think I've got it.

> [*He goes out hurriedly. And* BARTHWICK, *placing a chair, motions to the visitor to sit; then, with pursed lips, he stands and eyes her fixedly. She sits, and steals a look at him; then turns away, and, drawing up her veil, stealthily wipes her eyes. And* JACK *comes back.*

JACK. [*Ruefully holding out the empty reticule.*] Is that the thing? I've looked all over—I can't find the purse anywhere. Are you sure it was there?

UNKNOWN. [*Tearfully.*] Sure? Of course I'm sure. A crimson silk purse. It was all the money I had.

JACK. I really am awfully sorry—my head's so jolly bad. I've asked the butler, but he hasn't seen it.

UNKNOWN. I *must* have my money——

JACK. Oh! Of course—that'll be all right; I'll see that that's all right. How much?

UNKNOWN. [*Sullenly.*] Seven pounds—twelve—it's all I've got in the world.

JACK. That'll be all right; I'll—send you a—cheque.

UNKNOWN. [*Eagerly.*] No; now, please. Give me what was in my purse; I've got to pay my rent this morning. They won't give me another day; I'm a fortnight behind already.

JACK. [*Blankly.*] I'm awfully sorry; I really haven't a penny in my pocket.

[*He glances stealthily at* BARTHWICK.

UNKNOWN. [*Excitedly.*] Come, I say you must— it's my money, and you took it. I'm not going away without it. They'll turn me out of my place.

JACK. [*Clasping his head.*] But I can't give you what I haven't got. Don't I tell you I haven't a beastly penny?

UNKNOWN. [*Tearing at her handkerchief.*] Oh! do give it me! [*She puts her hands together in appeal; then, with sudden fierceness.*] If you don't I'll summons you. It's stealing, that's what it is!

BARTHWICK. [*Uneasily.*] One moment, please. As a matter of—er— principle, I shall settle this claim. [*He produces money.*] Here is eight pounds; the extra will cover the value of the purse and your cab fares. I need make no comment—no thanks are necessary.

> [*Touching the bell, he holds the door ajar in silence. The Unknown lady stores the money in her reticule, she looks from* JACK *to* BARTHWICK, *and her face is quivering faintly with a smile. She hides it with her hand, and steals away. Behind her* BARTH-WICK *shuts the door.*

BARTHWICK. [*With solemnity.*] H'm! This is a nice thing to happen!

JACK. [*Impersonally.*] What awful luck!

BARTHWICK. So this is the way that forty pounds has gone! One thing after another! Once more I should like to know where you'd have been if it hadn't been for me! You don't seem to have any principles. You —you're one of those who are a nuisance to society; you—you're dangerous! What your mother would say I don't know. Your conduct, as far as I can see, is absolutely unjustifiable. It's—it's criminal. Why, a poor man who behaved as you've done . . . d'you think he'd have any mercy shown him? What you want is a good lesson. You and your sort are—[*he speaks with feeling*]—a nuisance to the community. Don't ask me to help you next time. You're not fit to be helped.

JACK. [*Turning upon his sire, with unexpected fierceness.*] All right, I won't then, and see how you like it. You wouldn't have helped me this time, I know, if you hadn't been scared the thing would get into the papers. Where are the cigarettes?

BARTHWICK. [*Regarding him uneasily.*] Well—I'll
say no more about it.   [*He rings the bell.*] I'll pass it
over for this once, but——   [MARLOW *comes in*
You can clear away.

[*He hides his face behind the " Times."*

JACK. [*Brightening.*] I say, Marlow, where are the
cigarettes ?

MARLOW. I put the box out with the whisky last
night, sir, but this morning I can't find it anywhere.

JACK. Did you look in my room ?

MARLOW. Yes, sir ; I've looked all over the house.
I found two Nestor ends in the tray this morning,
so you must have been smokin' last night, sir.
[*Hesitating.*] I'm really afraid some one's purloined
the box.

JACK. [*Uneasily.*] Stolen it !

BARTHWICK. What's that ? The cigarette-box ! Is
anything else missing ?

MARLOW. No, sir ; I've been through the plate.

BARTHWICK. Was the house all right this morning ?
None of the windows open ?

MARLOW. No, sir.   [*Quietly to* JACK.]   You left
your latchkey in the door last night, sir.

[*He hands it back, unseen by* BARTHWICK.
JACK. Tst !

BARTHWICK. Who's been in the room this morning ?

MARLOW. Me and Wheeler, and Mrs. Jones is all,
sir, as far as I know.

BARTHWICK. Have you asked Mrs. Barthwick ? [*To*
JACK.]   Go and ask your mother if she's had it;

ask her to look and see if she's missed anything else.   [JACK *goes upon this mission.*
Nothing is more disquieting than losing things like this.

MARLOW. No, sir.

BARTHWICK. Have you any suspicions?

MARLOW. No, sir.

BARTHWICK. This Mrs. Jones—how long has she been working here?

MARLOW. Only this last month, sir.

BARTHWICK. What sort of person?

MARLOW. I don't know much about her, sir; seems a very quiet, respectable woman.

BARTHWICK. Who did the room this morning?

MARLOW. Wheeler and Mrs. Jones, sir.

BARTHWICK. [*With his forefinger upraised.*] Now, was this Mrs. Jones in the room alone at any time?

MARLOW. [*Expressionless.*] Yes, sir.

BARTHWICK. How do you know that?

MARLOW. [*Reluctantly.*] I found her here, sir.

BARTHWICK. And has Wheeler been in the room alone?

MARLOW. No, sir, she's not, sir. I should say, sir, that Mrs. Jones seems a very honest——

BARTHWICK. [*Holding up his hand.*] I want to know this: Has this Mrs. Jones been here the whole morning?

MARLOW. Yes, sir—no, sir—she stepped over to the greengrocer's for cook.

BARTHWICK. H'm! Is she in the house now?

MARLOW. Yes, sir.

BARTHWICK. Very good. I shall make a point of clearing this up. On principle I shall make a point of fixing the responsibility ; it goes to the foundations of security. In all your interests——

MARLOW. Yes, sir.

BARTHWICK. What sort of circumstances is this Mrs. Jones in ? Is her husband in work ?

MARLOW. I believe not, sir.

BARTHWICK. Very well. Say nothing about it to any one. Tell Wheeler not to speak of it, and ask Mrs. Jones to step up here.

MARLOW. Very good, sir.

> [MARLOW *goes out, his face concerned ; and* BARTHWICK *stays, his face judicial and a little pleased, as befits a man conducting an inquiry.* MRS. BARTHWICK *and her son come in.*

BARTHWICK. Well, my dear, you've not seen it, I suppose ?

MRS. BARTHWICK. No. But what an extraordinary thing, John ! Marlow, of course, is out of the question. I'm certain none of the maids——As for cook!

BARTHWICK. Oh, cook !

MRS. BARTHWICK. Of course ! It's perfectly detestable to me to suspect anybody.

BARTHWICK. It is not a question of one's feelings. It's a question of justice. On principle——

MRS. BARTHWICK. I shouldn't be a bit surprised if the charwoman knew something about it. It was Laura who recommended her.

BARTHWICK. [*Judicially.*] I am going to have Mrs. Jones up. Leave it to me; and—er—remember that nobody is guilty until they're proved so. I shall be careful. I have no intention of frightening her; I shall give her every chance. I hear she's in poor circumstances. If we are not able to do much for them we are bound to have the greatest sympathy with the poor. [MRS. JONES *comes in.* [*Pleasantly.*] Oh! good morning, Mrs. Jones.

MRS. JONES. [*Soft, and even, unemphatic.*] Good morning, sir! Good morning, ma'am!

BARTHWICK. About your husband—he's not in work, I hear?

MRS. JONES. No, sir; of course he's not in work just now.

BARTHWICK. Then I suppose he's earning nothing.

MRS. JONES. No, sir, he's not earning anything just now, sir.

BARTHWICK. And how many children have you?

MRS. JONES. Three children; but of course they don't eat very much, sir. [*A little silence.*

BARTHWICK. And how old is the eldest?

MRS. JONES. Nine years old, sir.

BARTHWICK. Do they go to school?

MRS. JONES. Yes, sir, they all three go to school every day.

BARTHWICK. [*Severely.*] And what about their food when you're out at work.

MRS. JONES. Well, sir, I have to give them their dinner to take with them. Of course I'm not always able to give them anything; sometimes I have to send them without; but my husband is very good about the children when he's in work.   But when he's not in work of course he's a very difficult man.

BARTHWICK. He drinks, I suppose?

MRS. JONES. Yes, sir. Of course I can't say he doesn't drink, because he does.

BARTHWICK. And I suppose he takes all your money?

MRS. JONES. No, sir, he's very good about my money, except when he's not himself, and then, of course, he treats me very badly.

BARTHWICK. Now what is he—your husband?

MRS. JONES. By profession, sir, of course he's a groom.

BARTHWICK. A groom! How came he to lose his place?

MRS. JONES. He lost his place a long time ago, sir, and he's never had a very long job since; and now, of course, the motor-cars are against him.

BARTHWICK. When were you married to him, Mrs. Jones?

MRS. JONES. Eight years ago, sir—that was in——

MRS. BARTHWICK. [Sharply] Eight? You said the eldest child was nine.

MRS. JONES. Yes, ma'am; of course that was why he lost his place. He didn't treat me rightly, and of course his employer said he couldn't keep him because of the example.

BARTHWICK.   You mean he—ahem——

MRS. JONES. Yes, sir; and of course after he lost his place he married me.

MRS. BARTHWICK. You actually mean to say you—you were——

BARTHWICK. My dear——

MRS. BARTHWICK. [*Indignantly.*] How disgraceful!

BARTHWICK. [*Hurriedly.*] And where are you living now, Mrs. Jones?

MRS. JONES. We've not got a home, sir. Of course we've been obliged to put away most of onr things.

BARTHWICK. Put your things away! You mean to —to—er—to pawn them?

MRS. JONES. Yes, sir, to put them away. We're living in Merthyr Street—that is close by here, sir—at No. 34. We just have the one room.

BARTHWICK. And what do you pay a week?

MRS. JONES. We pay six shillings a week, sir, for a furnished room.

BARTHWICK. And I suppose you're behind in the rent?

MRS. JONES. Yes, sir, we're a little behind in the rent.

BARTHWICK. But *you're* in good work, aren't you?

MRS. JONES. Well, sir, I have a day in Stamford Place Thursdays. And Mondays and Wednesdays and Fridays I come here. But to-day, of course, is a half-day, because of yesterday's Bank Holiday.

BARTHWICK. I see; four days a week, and you get half a crown a day, is that it?

MRS. JONES. Yes, sir, and my dinner; but sometimes it's only half a day, and that's eighteenpence.

BARTHWICK. And when your husband earns anything he spends it in drink, I suppose?

MRS. JONES. Sometimes he does, sir, and sometimes he gives it to me for the children. Of course he would work if he could get it, sir, but it seems there are a great many people out of work.

BARTHWICK. Ah! Yes. We—er—won't go into that. [Sympathetically.] And how about your work here? Do you find it hard?

MRS. JONES. Oh! no, sir, not very hard, sir; except of course, when I don't get my sleep at night.

BARTHWICK. Ah! And you help do all the rooms? And sometimes, I suppose, you go out for cook?

MRS. JONES. Yes, sir.

BARTHWICK. And you've been out this morning?

MRS. JONES. Yes, sir, of course I had to go to the greengrocer's.

BARTHWICK. Exactly. So your husband earns nothing? And he's a bad character.

MRS. JONES. No, sir, I don't say that, sir. I think there's a great deal of good in him; though he does treat me very bad sometimes. And of course I don't like to leave him, but I think I ought to, because really I hardly know how to stay with him. He often raises his hand to me. Not long ago he gave me a blow here [touches her breast] and I can

C

feel it now.   So I think I ought to leave him, don't *you*, sir ?

BARTHWICK. Ah ! I can't help you there. It's a very serious thing to leave your husband.   Very serious thing.

MRS. JONES. Yes, sir, of course I'm afraid of what he might do to me if I were to leave him ; he can be so very violent.

BARTHWICK. H'm ! Well, that I can't pretend to say anything about.   It's the bad principle I'm speaking of—

MRS. JONES. Yes, sir ; I know nobody can help me. I know I must decide for myself, and of course I know that he has a very hard life.   And he's fond of the children, and it's very hard for him to see them going without food.

BARTHWICK. [*Hastily.*] Well—er—thank you, I just wanted to hear about you.   I don't think I need detain you any longer, Mrs.—Jones.

MRS. JONES. No, sir, thank you, sir.

BARTHWICK. Good morning, then.

MRS. JONES. Good morning, sir ; good morning, ma'am.

BARTHWICK. [*Exchanging glances with his wife.*] By the way, Mrs. Jones—I think it is only fair to tell you, a silver cigarette box—er—is missing.

MRS. JONES. [*Looking from one face to the other.*] I am very sorry, sir.

BARTHWICK. Yes ; you have not seen it, I suppose ?

MRS. JONES. [*Realising that suspicion is upon her ;*

with an uneasy movement.]   Where was it, sir; if you please, sir?

BARTHWICK. [*Evasively.*]   Where did Marlow say? Er—in this room, yes, in *this* room.

MRS. JONES. No, sir, I haven't seen it—of course if I'd seen it I should have noticed it.

BARTHWICK. [*Giving her a rapid glance.*]   You—you are sure of that?

MRS. JONES. [*Impassively.*]   Yes, sir. [*With a slow nodding of her head.*]   I have not seen it, and of course I *don't* know where it is.

[*She turns and goes quietly out.*

BARTHWICK. H'm!

[*The three* BARTHWICKS *avoid each other's glances.*]

The curtain falls.

ACT II

SCENE I

The JONES' *lodgings, Merthyr Street, at half-past two o'clock.*

The bare room, with tattered oilcloth and damp, distempered walls, has an air of tidy wretchedness. On the bed lies JONES, *half-dressed ; his coat is thrown across his feet, and muddy boots are lying on the floor close by. He is asleep. The door is opened and* MRS. JONES *comes in, dressed in a pinched black jacket and old black sailor hat; she carries a parcel wrapped up in " The Times." She puts her parcel down, unwraps an apron, half a loaf, two onions, three potatoes, and a tiny piece of bacon. Taking a teapot from the cupboard, she rinses it, shakes into it some powdered tea out of a screw of paper, puts it on the hearth, and sitting in a wooden chair quietly begins to cry.*

JONES. [*Stirring and yawning.*] That you ? What's the time ?

MRS. JONES. [*Drying her eyes, and in her usual voice.*] Half-past two.

JONES. What you back so soon for ?

MRS. JONES. I only had the half-day to-day, Jem.

JONES. [*On his back, and in a drowsy voice.*] Got anything for dinner?

MRS. JONES. Mrs. Barthwick's cook gave me a little bit of bacon. I'm going to make a stew. [*She prepares for cooking.*] There's fourteen shillings owing for rent, James, and of course I've only got two and fourpence. They'll be coming for it to-day.

JONES. [*Turning towards her on his elbow.*] Let 'em come and find my surprise packet. I've had enough o' this tryin' for work. Why should I go round and round after a job like a bloomin' squirrel in a cage. "Give us a job, sir "—" Take a man on "—" Got a wife and three children." Sick of it I am! I'd sooner lie here and rot. " Jones, you come and join the demonstration; come and 'old a flag, and listen to the ruddy orators, and go 'ome as empty as you came." There's some that seems to like *that*—the sheep! When I go seekin' for a job now, and see the brutes lookin' me up an' down, it's like a thousand serpents in me. I'm not arskin' for any treat. A man wants to sweat hisself silly and not allowed— that's a rum start, ain't it? A man wants to sweat his soul out to keep the breath in him and ain't allowed—that's justice—that's freedom and all the rest of it! [*He turns his face towards the wall.*] You're so milky mild; you don't know what goes on inside o' me. I'm done with the silly game. If they want me, let 'em come for me!

[MRS. JONES *stops cooking and stands unmoving
    at the table.*]

I've tried and done with it, I tell you. I've never
been afraid of what's before *me*.   You mark my words
—if you think they've broke my spirit, you're mistook.
I'll lie and rot sooner than arsk 'em again.   What
makes you stand like that—you long-sufferin', Gawd-
forsaken image—that's why I can't keep my hands
off you. So now you know. Work ! You can work,
but you haven't the spirit of a louse !

MRS. JONES. [*Quietly.*] You talk more wild sometimes when you're yourself, James, than when you're
not. If you don't get work, how are we to go on ?
They won't let us stay here ; they're looking to their
money to-day, I know.

JONES. I see this Barthwick o' yours every day
goin' down to Pawlyment snug and comfortable to
talk his silly soul out ; an' I see that young calf, his
son, swellin' it about, and goin' on the razzle-dazzle.
Wot 'ave they done that makes 'em any better than
wot I am ? They never did a day's work in their
lives.   I see 'em day after day——

MRS. JONES. And I wish you wouldn't come after
me like that, and hang about the house. You don't
seem able to keep away at all, and whatever you
do it for I can't think, because of course they notice
it.

JONES. I suppose I may go where I like. Where
may I go ? The other day I went to a place in the
Edgware Road. "Gov'nor," I says to the boss,

"take me on," I says. "I 'aven't done a stroke o'
work not these two months; it takes the heart out
of a man," I says; "I'm one to work; I'm not afraid
of anything you can give me!" "My good man,"
'e says, "I've had thirty of you here this morning.
I took the first two," he says, "and that's all I want."
"Thank you, then rot the world!" I says. "Blas-
phemin'," he says, "is not the way to get a job.
Out you go, my lad!" [*He laughs sardonically.*] Don't
you raise your voice because you're starvin'; don't yer
even think of it; take it lyin' down! Take it like a
sensible man, carn't you? And a little way down
the street a lady says to me: [*Pinching his voice*]
"D'you want to earn a few pence, my man?" and
gives me her dog to 'old outside a shop—fat as a
butler 'e was—tons o' meat had gone to the makin'
of *him*. It did 'er good, it did, made 'er feel 'erself
that *charitable*, but I see 'er lookin' at the copper
standin' alongside o' me, for fear I should make off
with 'er bloomin' fat dog. [*He sits on the edge of the
bed and puts a boot on. Then looking up.*] What's in
that head o' yours? [*Almost pathetically.*] Carn't you
speak for once?

> [*There is a knock, and* MRS. SEDDON, *the landlady,
> appears, an anxious, harassed, shabby woman
> in working clothes.*]

MRS. SEDDON. I thought I 'eard you come in, Mrs.
Jones. I've spoke to my 'usband, but he says he
really can't afford to wait another day.

JONES. [*With scowling jocularity.*] Never you mind

what your 'usband says, you go your own way like a
proper independent woman.   Here, Jenny, chuck
her that.

> [*Producing a sovereign from his trousers pocket,
> he throws it to his wife, who catches it in
> her apron with a gasp.   JONES resumes the
> lacing of his boots.*

MRS. JONES. [*Rubbing the sovereign stealthily.*] I'm
very sorry we're so late with it, and of course it's
fourteen shillings, so if you've got six that will be
right.

> [*MRS. SEDDON takes the sovereign and fumbles
> for the change.*

JONES. [*With his eyes fixed on his boots.*] Bit of a
surprise for yer, ain't it?

MRS. SEDDON. Thank you, and I'm sure I'm very
much obliged.   [*She does indeed appear surprised.*]
I'll bring you the change.

JONES. [*Mockingly.*] Don't mention it.

MRS. SEDDON. Thank you, and I'm sure I'm very
much obliged.   [*She slides away.*

> [*MRS. JONES gazes at JONES, who is still lacing
> up his boots.*

JONES. I've had a bit of luck. [*Pulling out the crimson purse and some loose coins.*] Picked up a purse—
seven pound and more.

MRS. JONES. Oh, James!

JONES. Oh, James!   What about Oh, James!   I
picked it up I tell you.   This is lost property, this
is!

Mrs. Jones. But isn't there a name in it, or something?

Jones. Name? No, there ain't no name. This don't belong to such as 'ave visitin' cards. This belongs to a perfec' lidy. Tike an' smell it. [*He pitches her the purse, which she puts gently to her nose.*] Now, you tell me what I ought to have done. You tell me that. You can always tell me what I ought to ha' done, can't yer?

Mrs. Jones. [*Laying down the purse.*] I can't say what you ought to have done, James. Of course the money wasn't yours; you've taken somebody else's money.

Jones. Finding's keeping. I'll take it as wages for the time I've gone about the streets asking for what's my rights. I'll take it for what's *overdue*, d'ye hear? [*With strange triumph.*] I've got money in my pocket, my girl.

> [Mrs. Jones *goes on again with the preparation of the meal,* Jones *looking at her furtively.*]

Money in my pocket! And I'm not goin' to waste it. With this 'ere money I'm goin' to Canada. I'll let you have a pound. [*A silence.*] You've often talked of leavin' me. You've often told me I treat you badly —well I 'ope you'll be glad when I'm gone.

Mrs. Jones. [*Impassively.*] You *have* treated me very badly, James, and of course I can't prevent your going; but I can't tell whether I shall be glad when you're gone.

Jones. It'll change my luck. I've 'ad nothing but

SC. I   THE SILVER BOX   43

bad luck since I first took up with you. [*More softly.*]
And you've 'ad no bloomin' picnic.

MRS. JONES. Of course it would have been better
for us if we had never met. We weren't meant for
each other. But you're set against me, that's what
you are, and you *have* been for a long time. And
you treat me so badly, James, going after that Rosie
and all. You don't ever seem to think of the children
that I've had to bring into the world, and of all the
trouble I've had to keep them, and what'll become of
them when you're gone.

JONES. [*Crossing the room gloomily.*] If you think I
want to leave the little beggars you're bloomin' well
mistaken.

MRS. JONES. Of course I know you're fond of them.

JONES. [*Fingering the purse, half angrily.*] Well, then,
you stow it, old girl.   The kids'll get along better with
you than when I'm here. If I'd ha' known as much
as I do now, I'd never ha' had one o' them. What's
the use o' bringin' 'em into a state o' things like this ?
It's a crime, that's what it is ; but you find it out too
late ; that's what's the matter with this 'ere world.

[*He puts the purse back in his pocket.*

MRS. JONES. Of course it would have been better
for them, poor little things ; but they're your own
children, and I wonder at you talkin' like that. I
should miss them dreadfully if I was to lose them.

JONES. [*Sullenly.*] An' you ain't the only one.   If I
make money out there—— [*Looking up, he sees her shak-
ng out his coat—in a changed voice*] Leave that coat alone!

[*The silver box drops from the pocket, scattering the cigarettes upon the bed. Taking up the box she stares at it ; he rushes at her and snatches the box away.*

MRS. JONES. [*Cowering back against the bed.*] Oh, Jem! oh, Jem!

JONES. [*Dropping the box on to the table.*] You mind what you're sayin'! When I go out I'll take and chuck it in the water along with that there purse. I 'ad it when I was in liquor, and for what you do when you're in liquor you're not responsible—and that's Gawd's truth as you ought to know. I don't want the thing—I won't have it. I took it out o' spite. I'm no thief, I tell you; and don't you call me one, or it'll be the worse for you.

MRS. JONES. [*Twisting her apron strings.*] It's Mr. Barthwick's! You've taken away my reputation. Oh, Jem, whatever made you?

JONES. What d'you mean?

MRS. JONES. It's been missed ; they think it's me. Oh! whatever made you do it, Jem?

JONES. I tell you I was in liquor. I don't want it ; what's the good of it to me? If I were to pawn it they'd only nab me. I'm no thief. I'm no worse than wot that yonng Barthwick is ; he brought 'ome that purse that I picked up—a lady's purse— 'ad it off 'er in a row, kept sayin' 'e'd scored 'er off. Well, I scored 'im off. Tight as an owl 'e was! And d'you think anything'll happen to him?

MRS. JONES. [*As though speaking to herself.*] Oh, Jem! it's the bread out of our mouths!

JONES. Is it then? I'll make it hot for 'em yet. What about that purse? What about young Barthwick?

> [MRS. JONES *comes forward to the table and tries to take the box;* JONES *prevents her.*]

What do you want with that? You drop it, I say!

MRS. JONES. I'll take it back and tell them all about it.   [*She attempts to wrest the box from him.*

JONES. Ah, would yer?

> [*He drops the box, and rushes on her with a snarl. She slips back past the bed. He follows; a chair is overturned. The door is opened;* SNOW *comes in, a detective in plain clothes and bowler hat, with clipped moustaches.* JONES *drops his arms,* MRS. JONES *stands by the window gasping;* SNOW, *advancing swiftly to the table, puts his hand on the silver box.*

SNOW. Doin' a bit o' skylarkin'? Fancy this is what I'm after. J.B., the very same. [*He gets back to the door, scrutinising the crest and cypher on the box. To* MRS. JONES.] I'm a police officer. Are you Mrs. Jones?

MRS. JONES. Yes, sir.

SNOW. My instructions are to take you on a charge of stealing this box from J. Barthwick, Esquire, M.P., of 6, Rockingham Gate. Anything you say may be used against you. Well, missis?

MRS. JONES. [*In her quiet voice, still out of breath, her hand upon her breast.*] Of course I did *not* take it, sir. I never have taken anything that didn't belong to me ; and of course I know nothing about it.

SNOW. You were at the house this morning ; you did the room in which the box was left; you were alone in the room. I find the box 'ere. You say you didn't take it ?

MRS. JONES. Yes, sir, of course I say I did not take it, because I did *not*.

SNOW. Then how does the box come to be here ?

MRS. JONES. I would rather not say anything about it.

SNOW. Is this your husband ?

MRS. JONES.   Yes, sir, this is my husband, sir.

SNOW. Do you wish to say anything before I take her ?

> [JONES *remains silent, with his head bent down.*]

Well then, Missis. I'll just trouble you to come along with me quietly.

MRS. JONES. [*Twisting her hands.*] Of course I wouldn't say I hadn't taken it if I had—and I *didn't* take it, indeed I didn't. Of course I know appearances are against me, and I can't tell you what really happened. But my children are at school, and they'll be coming home—and I don't know what they'll do without me !

SNOW. Your 'usband'll see to them, don't you worry.   [*He takes the woman gently by the arm,*

JONES. You drop it—she's all right! [*Sullenly.*] I took the thing myself.

SNOW. [*Eycing him.*] There, there, it does you credit.   Come along, Missis.

JONES. [*Passionately.*] Drop it, I say, you blooming teck.   She's my wife ; she's a respectable woman. Take her if you dare !

SNOW. Now, now.   What's the good of this ?   Keep a civil tongue, and it'll be the better for all of us.

> [*He puts his whistle in his mouth and draws the woman to the door.*

JONES. [*With a rush.*] Drop her, and put up your 'ands, or I'll soon make yer.   You leave her alone, will yer !   Don't I tell yer, I took the thing myself !

SNOW. [*Blowing his whistle.*] Drop your hands, or I'll take you too.   Ah, would you ?

> [JONES, *closing, deals him a blow.   A Policeman in uniform appears ; there is a short struggle and* JONES *is overpowered.*   MRS. JONES *raises her hands and drops her face on them.*
>
> *The curtain falls.*

SCENE II

[*The* BARTHWICKS' *dining-room the same evening.   The* BARTHWICKS *are seated at dessert.*

MRS. BARTHWICK. John !   [*A silence broken by the cracking of nuts.*]   John !

BARTHWICK. I wish you'd speak about the nuts— they're uneatable. [*He puts one in his mouth.*

MRS. BARTHWICK. It's not the season for them. I called on the Holyroods.

[BARTHWICK *fills his glass with port.*

JACK. Crackers, please, dad.

[BARTHWICK *passes the crackers. His demeanour is reflective.*

MRS. BARTHWICK. Lady Holyrood has got very stout. I've noticed it coming for a long time.

BARTHWICK. [*Gloomily.*] Stout? [*He takes up the crackers—with transparent airiness.*] The Holyroods had some trouble with their servants, hadn't they?

JACK. Crackers, please, dad.

BARTHWICK. [*Passing the crackers.*] It got into the papers. The cook, wasn't it?

MRS. BARTHWICK. No, the lady's maid. I was talking it over with Lady Holyrood. The girl used to have her young man to see her.

BARTHWICK. [*Uneasily.*] I'm not sure they were wise——

MRS. BARTHWICK. My dear John, what are you talking about? How could there be any alternative? Think of the effect on the other servants!

BARTHWICK. Of course in principle — I wasn't thinking of that.

JACK. [*Maliciously.*] Crackers, please, dad.

[BARTHWICK *is compelled to pass the crackers.*

MRS. BARTHWICK. Lady Holyrood told me: "I had her up," she said; "I said to her, 'You'll leave

my house at once; I think your conduct disgraceful.
I can't tell, I don't know, and I don't wish to know,
what you were doing. I send you away on principle;
you need not come to me for a character.' And the
girl said: ' If you don't give me my notice, my lady,
I want a month's wages. I'm perfectly respectable.
I've done nothing.' ''—Done nothing !

BARTHWICK. H'm !

MRS. BARTHWICK. Servants have too much licence.
They hang together so terribly you never can tell
what they're really thinking; it's as if they were all
in a conspiracy to keep you in the dark. Even with
Marlow, you feel that he never lets you know what's
really in his mind. I hate that secretiveness; it de-
stroys all confidence. I feel sometimes I should like
to shake him.

JACK. Marlow's a most decent chap. It's simply
beastly every one knowing your affairs.

BARTHWICK. The less you say about that the better!

MRS. BARTHWICK. It goes all through the lower
classes. You can *not* tell when they are speaking the
truth. To-day when I was shopping after leaving
the Holyroods, one of these unemployed came up
and spoke to me. I suppose I only had twenty yards
or so to walk to the carriage, but he seemed to spring
up in the street.

BARTHWICK. Ah ! You must be very careful whom
you speak to in these days.

MRS. BARTHWICK. I didn't answer him, of course.
But I could see at once that he wasn't telling the truth.

D

BARTHWICK. [*Cracking a nut.*] There's one very good rule—look at their eyes.

JACK. Crackers, please, Dad.

BARTHWICK. [*Passing the crackers.*] If their eyes are straightforward I sometimes give them sixpence. It's against my principles, but it's most difficult to refuse. If you see that they're desperate, and dull, and shifty-looking, as so many of them are, it's certain to mean drink, or crime, or something unsatisfactory.

MRS. BARTHWICK. This man had dreadful eyes. He looked as if he could commit a murder. "I've 'ad nothing to eat to-day," he said. Just like that.

BARTHWICK. What was William about? He ought to have been waiting.

JACK. [*Raising his wineglass to his nose.*] Is this the '63, Dad?

[BARTHWICK, *holding his wine-glass to his eye, lowers it and passes it before his nose.*

MRS. BARTHWICK. I hate people that can't speak the truth. [*Father and son exchange a look behind their port.*] It's just as easy to speak the truth as not. *I've* always found it easy enough. It makes it impossible to tell what is genuine; one feels as if one were continually being taken in.

BARTHWICK. [*Sententiously.*] The lower classes are their own enemies. If they would only trust us, they would get on so much better.

MRS. BARTHWICK. But even then it's so often their own fault. Look at that Mrs. Jones this morning.

BARTHWICK. I only want to do what's right in that

matter.   I had occasion to see Roper this afternoon.
I mentioned it to him.   He's coming in this evening.
It all depends on what the detective says.   I've had
my doubts.   I've been thinking it over.

MRS. BARTHWICK. The woman impressed me most
unfavourably.   She seemed to have no shame.   That
affair she was talking about—she and the man when
they were young, so immoral!   And before you and
Jack!   I could have put her out of the room!

BARTHWICK. Oh!   I don't want to excuse them,
but in looking at these matters one must consider——

MRS. BARTHWICK. Perhaps you'll say the man's
employer was wrong in dismissing him?

BARTHWICK. Of course not.   It's not there that I
feel doubt.   What I ask myself is——

JACK. Port, please, Dad.

BARTHWICK. [*Circulating the decanter in religious
imitation of the rising and setting of the sun.*]   I ask
myself whether we are sufficiently careful in making
inquiries about people before we engage them,
especially as regards moral conduct.

JACK. Pass the port, please, Mother!

MRS. BARTHWICK. [*Passing it.*] My dear boy, aren't
you drinking too much?

[JACK *fills his glass.*

MARLOW. [*Entering.*] Detective Snow to see you,
sir.

BARTHWICK. [*Uneasily.*] Ah! say I'll be with him
in a minute.

Mrs. Barthwick. [*Without turning.*] Let him come in here, Marlow.

> [Snow *enters in an overcoat, his bowler hat in hand.*

Barthwick. [*Half rising.*] Oh! Good evening!

Snow. Good evening, sir; good evening, ma'am. I've called round to report what I've done, rather late, I'm afraid—another case took me away. [*He takes the silver box out of his pocket, causing a sensation in the* Barthwick *family.*] This is the identical article, I believe.

Barthwick. Certainly, certainly.

Snow. Havin' your crest and cypher, as you described to me, sir, I'd no hesitation in the matter.

Barthwick. Excellent. Will you have a glass of— [*he glances at the waning port*]—er—sherry—[*pours out sherry*]. Jack, just give Mr. Snow this.

> [Jack *rises and gives the glass to* Snow; *then, lolling in his chair, regards him indolently.*

Snow. [*Drinking off wine and putting down the glass.*] After seeing you I went round to this woman's lodgings, sir. It's a low neighbourhood, and I thought it as well to place a constable below—and not without 'e was wanted, as things turned out.

Barthwick. Indeed!

Snow. Yes, sir, I 'ad some trouble. I asked her to account for the presence of the article. She could give me no answer, except to deny the theft; so I took her into custody; then her husband came for me, so I was obliged to take him, too, for assault. He was

very violent on the way to the station—very violent
—threatened you and your son, and altogether he
was a handful, I can tell you.

MRS. BARTHWICK. What a ruffian he must be!

SNOW. Yes, ma'am, a rough customer.

JACK. [*Sipping his wine, bemused.*] Punch the beggar's head.

SNOW. Given to drink, as I understand, Sir.

MRS. BARTHWICK. It's to be hoped he will get a
severe punishment.

SNOW. The odd thing is, sir, that he persists in
sayin' he took the box himself.

BARTHWICK.   Took the box himself!   [*He smiles.*]
What does he think to gain by that?

SNOW. He says the young gentleman was intoxi-
cated last night—[JACK *stops the cracking of a nut, and
looks at Snow. BARTHWICK, losing his smile, has put
his wineglass down; there is a silence—*SNOW, *looking
from face to face, remarks*]—took him into the
house and gave him whisky; and under the influence of an empty stomach the man says he took the
box.

MRS. BARTHWICK. The impudent wretch!

BARTHWICK. D'you mean that he—er—intends to
put this forward to-morrow——

SNOW. That'll be his line, sir; but whether he's
endeavouring to shield his wife, or whether [*he looks
at* JACK) there's something in it, will be for the
magistrate to say.

MRS. BARTHWICK. [*Haughtily.*] Something in what?

I don't understand you. As if my son would bring a man like that into the house!

BARTHWICK. [*From the fireplace, with an effort to be calm.*] My son can speak for himself, no doubt.—Well, Jack, what do you say?

MRS. BARTHWICK. [*Sharply.*] What does he say? Why, of course, he says the whole story's stuff!

JACK. [*Embarrassed.*] Well, of course, I—of course, I don't know anything about it.

MRS. BARTHWICK. I should think not, indeed! [*To* SNOW.] The man is an audacious Ruffian!

BARTHWICK. [*Suppressing jumps.*] But in view of my son's saying there's nothing in this—this fable—will it be necessary to proceed against the man under the circumstances?

SNOW. We shall have to charge him with the assault, sir. It would be as well for your son to come down to the Court. There'll be a remand, no doubt. The queer thing is there was quite a sum of money found on him, and a crimson silk purse. [BARTHWICK *starts;* JACK *rises and sits down again.*] I suppose the lady hasn't missed her purse?

BARTHWICK. [*Hastily.*] Oh, no! Oh! No!

JACK. No!

MRS. BARTHWICK. [*Dreamily.*] No! [*To* SNOW.] I've been inquiring of the servants. This man *does* hang about the house. I shall feel much safer if he gets a good long sentence; I do think we ought to be protected against such ruffians.

BARTHWICK. Yes, yes, of course, on principle—but

in this case we have a number of things to think of.
[*To* Snow.] I suppose, as you say, the man *must* be
charged, eh?

Snow. No question about that, sir.

Barthwick. [*Staring gloomily at* Jack.] This prose-
cution goes very much against the grain with me.   I
have great sympathy with the poor.   In my position
I'm bound to recognise the distress there is amongst
them.   The condition of the people leaves much to
be desired.   D'you follow me?   I wish I could see
my way to drop it.

Mrs. Barthwick. [*Sharply.*] John! it's simply not
fair to other people.   It's putting property at the
mercy of any one who likes to take it.

Barthwick. [*Trying to make signs to her aside.*]
I'm not defending him, not at all.   I'm trying to
look at the matter broadly.

Mrs. Barthwick.   Nonsense, John, there's a time
for everything.

Snow. [*Rather sardonically.*] I might point out,
sir, that to withdraw the charge of stealing would
not make much differeuce, because the facts must
come out [*he looks significantly at* Jack] in reference
to the assault; and as I said that charge will have to
go forward.

Barthwick. [*Hastily.*] Yes, oh! exactly! It's entirely on the woman's account—entirely a matter of
my own private feelings.

Snow. If I were you, sir, I should let things
take their course.   It's not likely there'll be

much difficulty.   These things are very quick
settled.

BARTHWICK. [*Doubtfully.*] You think so—you think
so?

JACK. [*Rousing himself.*] I say, what shall I have
to swear to?

SNOW. That's best known to yourself, sir. [*Re-
treating to the door.*] Better employ a solicitor, sir,
in case anything should arise. We shall have the
butler to prove the loss of the article. You'll excuse
me going, I'm rather pressed to-night. The case
may come on any time after eleven. Good evening,
sir; good evening, ma'am. I shall have to produce
the box in court to-morrow, so if you'll excuse me,
sir, I may as well take it with me.

> [*He takes the silver box and leaves them with a
> little bow.*

> [BARTHWICK *makes a move to follow him, then
> dashing his hands beneath his coat tails,
> speaks with desperation.*

BARTHWICK. I do wish you'd leave me to manage
things myself. You *will* put your nose into matters
you know nothing of. A pretty mess you've made
of this!

MRS. BARTHWICK. [*Coldly.*] I don't in the least
know what you're talking about. If you can't
stand up for your rights, I can. I've no patience
with your principles, it's such nonsense.

BARTHWICK. Principles! Good Heavens! What
have principles to do with it for goodness' sake?

Don't you know that Jack was drunk last night!

JACK. Dad!

MRS. BARTHWICK. [*In horror rising.*] Jack!

JACK. Look here, mother—I had supper. Everybody does. I mean to say—you know what I mean —it's absurd to call it being drunk. At Oxford everybody gets a bit " on " sometimes——

MRS. BARTHWICK. Well I think it's most dreadful! If that is really what you do at Oxford——

JACK. [*Angrily.*] Well, why did you send me there? One must do as other fellows do. It's such nonsense, I mean, to call it being drunk. Of course I'm awfully sorry. I've had such a beastly headache all day.

BARTHWICK. Tcha! If you'd only had the common decency to remember what happened when you came in. Then we should know what truth there was in what this fellow says—as it is, it's all the most confounded darkness.

JACK. [*Staring as though at half-formed visions.*] I just get a—and then—it's gone——

MRS. BARTHWICK. Oh, Jack! do you mean to say you were so tipsy you can't even remember——

JACK. Look here, mother! Of course I remember I came—I must have come——

BARTHWICK. [*Unguardedly, and walking up and down.*] Tcha!—and that infernal purse! Good Heavens! It'll get into the papers. Who on earth could have foreseen a thing like this? Better to have lost a dozen cigarette boxes, and said nothing about it. [*To his wife.*] It's all your doing. I told you so from the first. I wish to goodness Roper would come !

MRS. BARTHWICK. [*Sharply.*] I don't know what you're talking about, John.

BARTHWICK. [*Turning on her.*] No, you—you—you don't know anything ! [*Sharply.*] Where the devil is Roper ? If he can see a way out of this he's a better man than I take him for. I defy *anyone* to see a way out of it. *I* can't.

JACK. Look here, don't excite Dad—I can simply say I was too beastly tired, and don't remember anything except that I came in and [*in a dying voice*] went to bed the same as usual.

BARTHWICK. Went to bed ? Who knows where you went—I've lost all confidence. For all I know you slept on the floor.

JACK. [*Indignantly.*] I didn't, I slept on the——

BARTHWICK. [*Sitting on the sofa.*] Who cares where you slept ; what does it matter if he mentions the —the—a perfect disgrace ?

MRS. BARTHWICK. *What ?* [*A silence.*] I *insist* on knowing.

JACK. Oh ! nothing——

MRS. BARTHWICK. Nothing ? What do you mean by nothing, Jack ? There's your father in such a state about it——

JACK. It's only my purse.

MRS. BARTHWICK. Your purse ! You know perfectly well you haven't got one.

JACK. Well, it was somebody else's—It was all a joke—I didn't want the beastly thing——

MRS. BARTHWICK. Do you mean that you had another person's purse, and that this man took it too?

BARTHWICK. Tcha! Of course he took it too! A man like that Jones will make the most of it. It'll get into the papers.

MRS. BARTHWICK. I don't understand. What on earth is all the fuss about? [*Bending over* JACK, *and softly*.) Jack now, tell me dear! Don't be afraid. What is it? Come!

JACK. Oh, don't mother!

MRS. BARTHWICK. But don't what, dear?

JACK. It was pure sport. I don't know how I got the thing. Of course I'd had a bit of a row—I didn't know what I was doing—I was—I was—well, you know—I suppose I must have pulled the bag out of her hand.

MRS. BARTHWICK. Out of her hand? Whose hand? What bag—whose bag?

JACK. Oh! I don't know—*her* bag—it belonged to —[*in a desperate and rising voice*] a woman.

MRS. BARTHWICK. A woman? *Oh! Jack! No!*

JACK. [*Jumping up.*] You *would* have it. I didn't want to tell you. It's not my fault.

> [*The door opens and* MARLOW *ushers in a man of middle age, inclined to corpulence, in evening dress. He has a ruddy, thin moustache, and dark, quick-moving little eyes. His eyebrows are Chinese.*

MARLOW. Mr. Roper, sir. *[He leaves the room.*

ROPER. *[With a quick look round.]* How do you do?

[But neither JACK *nor* MRS. BARTHWICK *make a sign.*

BARTHWICK. *[Hurrying.]* Thank goodness you've come, Roper. You remember what I told you this afternoon; we've just had the detective here.

ROPER. Got the box?

BARTHWICK. Yes, yes, but look here—it wasn't the charwoman at all; her drunken loafer of a husband took the things—he says that fellow there *[he waves his hand at* JACK, *who with his shoulder raised, seems trying to ward off a blow]* let him into the house last night. Can you imagine such a thing?

[Roper laughs.

BARTHWICK. *[With excited emphasis.]* It's no laughing matter, Roper. I told you about that business of Jack's too—don't you see—the brute took both the things—took that infernal purse. It'll get into the papers.

ROPER. *[Raising his eyebrows.]* H'm! The purse! Depravity in high life! What does your son say?

BARTHWICK. He remembers nothing. D——n! Did you ever see such a mess? It'll get into the papers.

MRS. BARTHWICK. *[With her hand across her eyes.]* ! it's not that——

*[*BARTHWICK *and* ROPER *turn and look at her.*

BARTHWICK. It's the idea of that woman—she's just heard——

> [ROPER *nods. And* MRS. BARTHWICK, *setting her lips, gives a slow look at* JACK, *and sits down at the table.*]

What on earth's to be done, Roper? A ruffian like this Jones will make all the capital he can out of that purse.

MRS. BARTHWICK. I don't believe that Jack took that purse.

BARTHWICK. What—when the woman came here for it this morning?

MRS. BARTHWICK. Here? She had the impudence? Why wasn't I told?

> [*She looks round from face to face—no one answers her, there is a pause.*

BARTHWICK. [*Suddenly.*] What's to be done, Roper?

ROPER. [*Quietly to* JACK.] I suppose you didn't leave your latch-key in the door?

JACK. [*Sullenly.*] Yes, I did.

BARTHWICK. Good heavens! What next?

MRS. BARTHWICK. I'm certain you never let that man into the house, Jack, it's a wild invention. I'm sure there's not a word of truth in it, Mr. Roper.

ROPER. [*Very suddenly*]. Where did you sleep last night?

JACK. [*Promptly.*] On the sofa, there—[*hesitating*] that is—I——

BARTHWICK. On the sofa? D'you mean to say you didn't go to bed?

JACK. [*Sullenly*] No.

BARTHWICK. If you don't remember anything, how can you remember that?

JACK. Because I woke up there in the morning.

MRS. BARTHWICK. Oh, Jack!

BARTHWICK. Good Gracious!

JACK. And Mrs. Jones saw me. I wish you wouldn't bait me so.

ROPER. Do you remember giving any one a drink?

JACK. By Jove, I do seem to remember a fellow with—a fellow with—— [*He looks at Roper.*] I say, d'you want me——?

ROPER. [*Quick as lightning.*] With a dirty face?

JACK. [*With illumination.*] I do—I distinctly remember his——

> [BARTHWICK *moves abruptly;* MRS. BARTHWICK *looks at* ROPER *angrily, and touches her son's arm.*

MRS. BARTHWICK. You don't remember, it's ridiculous! I don't believe the man was ever here at all.

BARTHWICK. You must speak the truth, if it *is* the truth. But if you *do* remember such a dirty business, I shall wash my hands of you altogether.

JACK. [*Glaring at them.*] Well, what the devil——

MRS. BARTHWICK. Jack!

JACK. Well, mother, I—I don't know what you *do* want.

MRS. BARTHWICK. We want you to speak the truth and say you never let this low man into the house.

BARTHWICK. Of course if you think that you really

gave this man whisky in that disgraceful way, and let him see what you'd been doing, and were in such a disgusting condition that you don't remember a word of it——

ROPER. [*Quick.*] I've no memory myself—never had.

BARTHWICK. [*Desperately.*] I don't know what you're to say.

ROPER [*To* JACK.] Say nothing at all! Don't put yourself in a false position. The man stole the things or the woman stole the things, you had nothing to do with it. You were asleep on the sofa.

MRS. BARTHWICK. Your leaving the latchkey in the door was quite bad enough, there's no need to mention anything else. [*Touching his forehead softly.*] My dear, how hot your head is!

JACK. But I want to know what I'm to do. [*Passionately.*] I won't be badgered like this.

[MRS. BARTHWICK *recoils from him.*

ROPER. [*Very quickly.*] You forget all about it. You were asleep.

JACK. Must I go down to the Court to-morrow?

ROPER. [*Shaking his head.*] No.

BARTHWICK. [*In a relieved voice.*] Is that so?

ROPER. Yes.

BARTHWICK. But *you'll* go, Roper.

ROPER. Yes.

JACK. [*With wan cheerfulness.*] Thanks, awfully! So long as I don't have to go. [*Putting his hand up to his head.*] I think if you'll excuse me—I've had a most beastly day. [*He looks from his father to his mother.*]

MRS. BARTHWICK. [*Turning quickly.*] Good night my boy.

JACK. Good-night, mother.

> [*He goes out.* MRS. BARTHWICK *heaves a sigh. There is a silence.*

BARTHWICK. He gets off too easily. But for my money that woman would have prosecuted him.

ROPER. You find money useful.

BARTHWICK. I've my doubts whether we ought to hide the truth——

ROPER. There'll be a remand.

BARTHWICK. What! D'you mean he'll have to *appear* on the remand?

ROPER. Yes.

BARTHWICK. H'm, I thought you'd be able to—— Look here, Roper, you *must* keep that purse out of the papers. [ROPER *fixes his little eyes on him and nods.*]

MRS. BARTHWICK. Mr. Roper, don't you think the magistrate ought to be told what sort of people these Joneses are; I mean about their immorality before they were married. I don't know if John told you.

ROPER. Afraid it's not material.

MRS. BARTHWICK. Not material?

ROPER. Purely private life! May have happened to the magistrate.

BARTHWICK. [*With a movement as if to shift a burden.*] Then you'll take the thing into your hands?

ROPER. If the gods are kind. [*He holds his hand out.*]

BARTHWICK. [*Shaking it dubiously.*]   Kind—eh? What? You going?

ROPER. Yes. I've another case, something like yours—most unexpected.

> [*He bows to* MRS. BARTHWICK *and goes out, followed by* BARTHWICK, *talking to the last.* MRS. BARTHWICK *at the table bursts into smothered sobs.* BARTHWICK *returns.*

BARTHWICK. [*To himself.*] There'll be a scandal !

MRS. BARTHWICK. [*Disguising her grief at once.*] I simply can't imagine what Roper means by making a joke of a thing like that !

BARTHWICK. [*Staring strangely.*] You ! You can't imagine anything ! You've no more imagination than a fly !

MRS. BARTHWICK. [*Angrily.*] You dare to tell me that I have no imagination.

BARTHWICK. [*Flustered.*] I—I'm upset. From beginning to end, the whole thing has been utterly against my principles.

MRS. BARTHWICK. Rubbish ! You haven't any ! Your principles are nothing in the world but sheer—fright !

BARTHWICK. [*Walking to the window.*] I've never been frightened in my life. You heard what Roper said. It's enough to upset any one when a thing like this happens. Everything one says and does seems to turn in one's mouth—it's—it's uncanny. It's not the sort of thing I've been accustomed to. [*As though stifling, he throws the window open. The faint sobbing of a child comes in.*] What's that ?

> [*They listen.*

E

Mrs. Barthwick. [*Sharply.*] I can't stand that crying. I must send Marlow to stop it. My nerves are all on edge. [*She rings the bell.*]

Barthwick. I'll shut the window; you'll hear nothing. [*He shuts the window. There is silence.*]

Mrs. Barthwick. [*Sharply.*] That's no good! It's on my nerves. Nothing upsets me like a child's crying. [Marlow *comes in.*] What's that noise of crying, Marlow? It sounds like a child.

Barthwick. It is a child. I can see it against the railings.

Marlow. [*Opening the window, and looking out— quietly.*] It's Mrs. Jones's little boy, ma'am; he came here after his mother.

Mrs. Barthwick. [*Moving quickly to the window.*] Poor little chap! John, we oughtn't to go on with this!

Barthwick. [*Sitting heavily in a chair.*] Ah! but it's out of our hands!

> [Mrs. Barthwick *turns her back to the window. There is an expression of distress on her face. She stands motionless, compressing her lips. The crying begins again.* Barthwick *covers his ears with his hands, and* Marlow *shuts the window. The crying ceases.*

> *The curtain falls.*

ACT III

*Eight days have passed, and the scene is a London Police
Court at one o'clock. A canopied seat of Justice is
surmounted by the lion and unicorn. Before the
fire a worn-looking* MAGISTRATE *is warming his
coat-tails, and staring at two little girls in faded blue
and orange rags, who are placed before the dock.
Close to the witness-box is a* RELIEVING OFFICER *in
an overcoat, and a short brown beard. Beside the little
girls stands a bald* POLICE CONSTABLE. *On the front
bench are sitting* BARTHWICK *and* ROPER, *and behind
them* JACK. *In the railed enclosure are seedy-looking
men and women. Some prosperous constables sit or
stand about.*

MAGISTRATE. [*In his paternal and ferocious voice, hissing
his s's.*] Now let us dispose of these young ladies.

USHER. Theresa Livens, Maud Livens.

       [*The bald* CONSTABLE *indicates the little girls
          who remain silent, disillusioned, inattentive.*

Relieving Officer !

       [*The* RELIEVING OFFICER *steps into the witness-box.*

USHER. The evidence you give to the Court shall
be the truth, the whole truth, and nothing but the
truth, so help you God ! Kiss the book '

                [*The book is kissed.*

RELIEVING OFFICER. [*In a monotone, pausing slightly at each sentence end, that his evidence may be inscribed.*] About ten o'clock this morning, your Worship, I found these two little girls in Blue Street, Pulham, crying outside a public-house. Asked where their home was, they said they had no home. Mother had gone away. Asked about their father. Their father had no work. Asked where they slept last night. At their aunt's. I've made inquiries, your Worship. The wife has broken up the home and gone on the streets. The husband is out of work and living in common lodging-houses. The husband's sister has eight children of her own, and says she can't afford to keep these little girls any longer.

MAGISTRATE. [*Returning to his seat beneath the canopy of Justice.*] Now, let me see. You say the mother is on the streets ; what evidence have you of that ?

RELIEVING OFFICER. I have the husband here, your Worship.

MAGISTRATE. Very well ; then let us see him.

[*There are cries of ' LIVENS." The MAGISTRATE leans forward, and stares with hard compassion at the little girls. LIVENS comes in. He is quiet, with grizzled hair, and a muffler for a collar. He stands beside the witness-box.*] And you are their father ? Now, why don't you keep your little girls at home. How is it you leave them to wander about the streets like this ?

LIVENS. I've got no home, your Worship. I'm

living from 'and to mouth. I've got no work ; and nothin' to keep them on.

MAGISTRATE. How is that ?

LIVENS. [*Ashamedly.*] My wife, she broke my 'ome up, and pawned the things.

MAGISTRATE. But what made you let her ?

LEVINS. Your Worship, I'd no chance to stop 'er she did it when I was out lookin' for work.

MAGISTRATE. Did you ill-treat her ?

LIVENS. [*Emphatically.*] I never raised my 'and to her in my life, your Worship.

MAGISTRATE. Then what was it—did she drink ?

LIVENS. Yes, your Worship.

MAGISTRATE. Was she loose in her behaviour ?

LIVENS. [*In a low voice.*] Yes, your Worship.

MAGISTRATE. And where is she now ?

LIVENS. I don't know, your Worship. She went off with a man, and after that I——

MAGISTRATE. Yes, yes. Who knows anything of her ? [*To the bald* CONSTABLE.] Is she known here ?

RELIEVING OFFICER. Not in this district, your Worship ; but I have ascertained that she is well known——

MAGISTRATE. Yes—yes ; we'll stop at that. Now [*To the Father*] you say that she has broken up your home, and left these little girls. What provision can you make for them ? You look a strong man.

LIVENS. So I am, your Worship. I'm willin' enough to work, but for the life of me I can't get anything to do.

MAGISTRATE. But have you tried?

LIVENS. I've tried everything, your Worship—I've tried my 'ardest.

MAGISTRATE. Well, well——   [*There is a silence.*

RELIEVING OFFICER. If your Worship thinks it's a case, my people are willing to take them.

MAGISTRATE. Yes, yes, I know; but I've no evidence that this man is not the proper guardian for his children.   [*He rises and goes back to the fire.*

RELIEVING OFFICER. The mother, your Worship, is able to get access to them.

MAGISTRATE. Yes, yes; the mother, of course, is an improper person to have anything to do with them. [*To the Father.*] Well, now what do you say?

LIVENS. Your Worship, I can only say that if I could get work I should be only too willing to provide for them. But what can I do, your Worship? Here I am obliged to live from 'and to mouth in these 'ere common lodging-houses. I'm a strong man—I'm willing to work—I'm half as alive again as some of 'em—but you see, your Worship, my 'air's turned a bit, owing to the fever—[*Touches his hair*]—and that's against me; and I don't seem to get a chance anyhow.

MAGISTRATE. Yes—yes. [*Slowly.*] Well, I think it's a case. [*Staring his hardest at the little girls.*] Now, are you willing that these little girls should be sent to a home?

LIVENS. Yes, your Worship, I should be very willing.

MAGISTRATE. Well, I'll remand them for a week. Bring them again to-day week; if I see no reason against it then, I'll make an order.

RELIEVING OFFICER. To-day week, your Worship

> [*The bald* CONSTABLE *takes the little girls out by the shoulders. The Father follows them. The* MAGISTRATE, *returning to his seat, bends over and talks to his* CLERK *inaudibly.*

BARTHWICK. [*Speaking behind his hand.*] A painfu case, Roper; very distressing state of things.

ROPER. Hundreds like this in the Police Courts.

BARTHWICK. Most distressing ! The more I see ot it, the more important this question of the condition of the people seems to become. I shall certainly make a point of taking up the cudgels in the House. I shall move——

> [*The* MAGISTRATE *ceases talking to his* CLERK.

CLERK. Remands

> BARTHWICK *stops abruptly. There is a stir and* MRS.
> JONES *comes in by the public door;* JONES, *ushered by policemen, comes from the prisoner's door. They file into the dock.*

CLERK. James Jones, Jane Jones.

USHER. Jane Jones

BARTHWICK. [*In a whisper.*] The purse—the purse *must* be kept out of it, Roper. Whatever happens you must keep that out of the papers.

> [ROPER *nods.*

BALD CONSTABLE. Hush !

> [MRS. JONES, *dressed in her thin, black, wispy dress, and black straw hat, stands motionless with hands crossed on the front rail of the dock. JONES leans against the back rail of the dock, and keeps half turning, glancing defiantly about him. He is haggard and unshaven.*

CLERK. [*Consulting with his papers.*] This is the case remanded from last Wednesday, sir. Theft of a silver cigarette box and assault on the police ; the two charges were taken together. Jane Jones James Jones !

MAGISTRATE. [*Staring.*] Yes, yes ; I remember.

CLERK. Jane Jones.

MRS. JONES. Yes, sir.

CLERK. Do you admit stealing a silver cigarette box valued at five pounds, ten shillings, from the house of John Barthwick, M.P., between the hours of 11 P.M. on Easter Monday and 8.45 A.M. on Easter Tuesday last ? Yes or no ?

MRS. JONES. [*In a low voice.*] No, sir, I do not, sir.

CLERK. James Jones ? Do you admit stealing a silver cigarette box valued at five pounds, ten shillings, from the house of John Barthwick, M.P., between the hours of 11 P.M. on Easter Monday and 8.45 A.M. on Easter Tuesday last. And further making an assault on the police when in the execution of their duty at 3 P.M. on Easter Tuesday ? Yes or no ?

JONES. [*Sullenly.*] Yes, but I've a lot to say about it.

MAGISTRATE. [*To the* CLERK.] Yes—yes. But how comes it that these two people are charged with the same offence? Are they husband and wife?

CLERK. Yes, sir. You remember you ordered a remand for further evidence as to the story of the male prisoner.

MAGISTRATE. Have they been in custody since?

CLERK. You released the woman on her own recognizances, sir.

MAGISTRATE. Yes, yes, this is the case of the silver box; I remember now. Well?

CLERK. Thomas Marlow.

> [*The cry of* "THOMAS MARLOW" *is repeated.* MARLOW *comes in, and steps into the witness-box, and is sworn. The silver box is handed up, and placed on the rail.*

CLERK. [*Reading from his papers.*] Your name is Thomas Marlow? Are you butler to John Barthwick, M.P., of 6, Rockingham Gate?

MARLOW. Yes, sir.

CLERK. Did you between 10.45 and 11 o'clock on the night of Easter Monday last place a silver cigarette box on a tray on the dining-room table at 6, Rockingham Gate? Is that the box?

MARLOW. Yes, sir.

CLERK. And did you miss the same at 8.45 on the following morning, on going to remove the tray?

MARLOW. Yes, sir.

CLERK. Is the female prisoner known to you?

[MARLOW *nods*.]

Is she the charwoman employed at 6, Rockingham Gate?   [*Again* MARLOW *nods*.]

Did you at the time of your missing the box find her in the room alone?

MARLOW. Yes, sir.

CLERK. Did you afterwards communicate the loss to your employer, and did he send you to the police station?

MARLOW. Yes, sir.

CLERK. [*To* MRS. JONES.] Have you anything to ask him?

MRS. JONES. No, sir, nothing, thank you, sir.

CLERK. [*To* JONES.] James Jones, have you anything to ask this witness?

JONES. I don't know 'im.

MAGISTRATE. Are you sure you put the box in the place you say at the time you say?

MARLOW. Yes, your Worship.

MAGISTRATE. Very well; then now let us have the officer.

[MARLOW *leaves the box, and* SNOW *goes into it*.

USHER. The evidence you give to the court shall be the truth, the whole truth, and nothing but the truth, so help you God.   [*The book is kissed*.

CLERK. [*Reading from his papers*.] Your name is Robert Snow? You are a detective in the X. B. division of the Metropolitan police force? According to instructions received did you on Easter Tuesday last proceed to the prisoner's lodgings at 34, Merthyr Street, St. Soames'?   And did you on entering see the box produced, lying on the table?

SNOW. Yes, sir.

CLERK. Is that the box?

SNOW. [*Fingering the box.*] Yes, sir.

CLERK. And did you thereupon take possession of it, and charge the female prisoner with theft of the box from 6, Rockingham Gate?   And did she deny the same?

SNOW. Yes, sir.

CLERK. Did you take her into custody?

SNOW. Yes, sir.

MAGISTRATE. What was her behaviour?

SNOW. Perfectly quiet, your Worship. She persisted in the denial.   That's all.

MAGISTRATE. Do you know her?

SNOW. No, your Worship.

MAGISTRATE. Is she known here?

BALD CONSTABLE. No, your Worship, they're neither of them known, we've nothing against them at all.

CLERK. [*To* MRS. JONES.] Have you anything to ask the officer?

MRS. JONES. No, sir, thank you, I've nothing to ask him.

MAGISTRATE. Very well then—go on.

CLERK. [*Reading from his papers.*] And while you were taking the female prisoner did the male prisoner interpose, and endeavour to hinder you in the execution of your duty, and did he strike you a blow?

SNOW. Yes, sir.

CLERK. And did he say, " You let her go, I took the box myself"?

SNOW. He did.

CLERK. And did you blow your whistle and obtain the assistance of another constable, and take him into custody?

SNOW. I did.

CLERK. Was he violent on the way to the station, and did he use bad language, and did he several times repeat that he had taken the box himself?

[SNOW *nods.*]

Did you thereupon ask him in what manner he had stolen the box? And did you understand him to say that he had entered the house at the invitation of young Mr. Barthwick

[BARTHWICK, *turning in his seat, frowns at* ROPER.]

after midnight on Easter Monday, and partaken of whisky, and that under the influence of the whisky he had taken the box?

SNOW. I did, sir.

CLERK. And was his demeanour throughout very violent?

SNOW. It *was* very violent.

JONES. [*Breaking in.*] Violent—of course it was! You put your 'ands on my wife when I kept tellin' you I took the thing myself,

MAGISTRATE. [*Hissing, with protruded neck.*] Now—you will have your chance of saying what you want to say presently. Have you anything to ask the officer?

JONES. [*Sullenly.*] No.

MAGISTRATE. Very well then. Now let us hear what the female prisoner has to say first.

MRS. JONES. Well, your Worship, of course I can only say what I've said all along, that I didn't take the box.

MAGISTRATE. Yes, but did you know that it was taken?

MRS. JONES. No, your Worship. And, of course, as to what my husband says, your Worship, I can't speak of my own knowledge. Of course, I know that he came home very late on the Monday night. It was past one o'clock when he came in, and he was not himself at all.

MAGISTRATE. Had he been drinking?

MRS. JONES. Yes, your Worship.

MAGISTRATE. And was he drunk?

MRS. JONES. Yes, your Worship, he was almost quite drunk.

MAGISTRATE And did he say anything to you?

MRS. JONES. No, your Worship, only to call me names. And of course in the morning when I got up and went to work he was asleep. And I don't know anything more about it until I came home again. Except that Mr. Barthwick—that's my employer, your Worship—told me the box was missing.

MAGISTRATE. Yes, yes.

MRS. JONES. But of course when I was shaking out my husband's coat the cigarette-box fell out and all the cigarettes were scattered on the bed.

MAGISTRATE. You say all the cigarettes were scattered on the bed? [*To* SNOW.] Did you see the cigarettes scattered on the bed?

SNOW. No, your Worship, I did not.

MAGISTRATE. You see he says he didn't see them.

JONES. Well, they were there for all that.

SNOW. I can't say, your Worship, that I had the opportunity of going round the room; I had all my work cut out with the male prisoner.

MAGISTRATE. [*To* MRS. JONES.] Well, what more have you to say?

MRS. JONES. Of course when I saw the box, your Worship, I was dreadfully upset, and I couldn't think why he had done such a thing; when the officer came we were having words about it, because it is ruin to me, your Worship, in my profession, and I have three little children dependent on me.

MAGISTRATE. [*Protruding his neck.*] Yes—yes—but what did he say to you?

MRS. JONES. I asked him whatever came over him to do such a thing—and he said it was the drink. He said that he had had too much to drink, and something came over him. And of course, your Worship, he had had very little to eat all day, and the drink does go to the head when you have not had enough to eat. Your Worship may not know, but it is the truth. And I would like to say that all through his married life I have never known him to do such a thing before, though we have passed through great hardships and [*speaking with soft emphasis*] I am quite sure he would not have done it if he had been himself at the time.

MAGISTRATE. Yes, yes. But don't you know that that is no excuse?

MRS. JONES. Yes, your Worship. I know that it is no excuse.

> [*The* MAGISTRATE *leans over and parleys with his* CLERK.

JACK. [*Leaning over from his seat behind.*] I say, Dad——

BARTHWICK. Tsst! [*Sheltering his mouth he speaks to* ROPER.] Roper, you had better get up now and say that considering the circumstances and the poverty of the prisoners, we have no wish to proceed any further, and if the magistrate would deal with the case as one of disorder only on the part of——

BALD CONSTABLE. Hssshh!

> [ROPER *shakes his head*.

MAGISTRATE. Now, supposing what you say and what your husband says is true, what I have to consider is—how did he obtain access to this house, and were you in any way a party to his obtaining access? You are the charwoman employed at the house?

MRS. JONES. Yes, your Worship, and of course if I had let him into the house it would have been very wrong of me ; and I have never done such a thing in any of the houses where I have been employed.

MAGISTRATE. Well—so you say.   Now let us hear what story the male prisoner makes of it.

JONES. [*Who leans with his arms on the dock behind, speaks in a slow, sullen voice.*] Wot I say is wot my wife says.   I've never been 'ad up in a police-court before, an' I can prove I took it when in liquor.   I told her, an' she can tell you the same, that I was goin' to throw the thing into the water sooner then 'ave it on my mind.

MAGISTRATE. But how did you get into the *house* ?

JONES. I was passin.'   I was goin' 'ome from the " Goat and Bells."

MAGISTRATE. The " Goat and Bells,"—what is that ?   A public-house ?

JONES. Yes, at the corner.   It was Bank 'oliday, an' I'd 'ad a drop to drink.   I see this young Mr. Barthwick tryin' to find the keyhole on the wrong side of the door.

MAGISTRATE. Well ?

JONES. [*Slowly and with many pauses.*] Well—I 'elped 'im to find it—drunk as a lord 'e was.   He goes on, an' comes back again, and says, I've got nothin' for you, 'e says, but come in an' 'ave a drink.   So I went in just as you might 'ave done yourself.   We 'ad a drink o' whisky just as you might have 'ad, 'nd young Mr. Barthwick says to me, " Take a drink 'nd a smoke.   Take anything you like, 'e says.   And then he went to sleep on the sofa.   I 'ad some more whisky—an' I 'ad a smoke—and I 'ad some more whisky—an' I carn't tell yer what 'appened after that.

MAGISTRATE. Do you mean to say you were so drunk that you can remember nothing?

JACK. [*Softly to his father.*] I say, that's exactly what——

BARTHWICK. Tssh!

JONES. That's what I do mean.

MAGISTRATE. And yet you say you stole the box?

JONES. I never stole the box. I took it.

MAGISTRATE. [*Hissing, with protruded neck.*] You did not steal it—you took it. Did it belong to you—what is that but stealing?

JONES. I took it.

MAGISTRATE. You took it—you took it away from their house and you took it to your house——

JONES. [*Sullenly breaking in.*] I ain't got a house.

MAGISTRATE. Very well, let us hear what this young man Mr.—Mr. Barthwick—has to say to your story.

> [SNOW *leaves the witness-box.   The* BALD CON-
> STABLE *beckons* JACK, *who, clutching his hat,
> goes into the witness-box.* ROPER *moves to
> the table set apart for his profession.*

SWEARING CLERK. The evidence you give to the Court shall be the truth, the whole truth, and nothing but the truth, so help you God. Kiss the book.

> [*The Book is kissed.*

ROPER. [*Examining.*] What is your name?

F

JACK [*In a low voice.*] John Barthwick, Junior.

[*The* CLERK *writes it down.*

ROPER. Where do you live ?

JACK. At 6, Rockingham Gate.

[*All his answers are recorded by the Clerk.*

ROPER. You are the son of the owner ?

JACK. [*In a very low voice.*] Yes.

ROPER. Speak up, please. Do you know the prisoner ?

JACK. [*Looking at the* JONESES, *in a low voice.*] I've seen Mrs. Jones. I—[*in a loud voice*] don't know the man.

JONES. Well, I know you !

BALD CONSTABLE. Hssh !

ROPER. Now, did you come in late on the night of Easter Monday ?

JACK. Yes.

ROPER. And did you by mistake leave your latch-key in the door ?

JACK. Yes.

MAGISTRATE. Oh ! You left your latchkey in the door ?

ROPER. And is that all you can remember about your coming in ?

JACK. [*In a loud voice.*] Yes, it is.

MAGISTRATE. Now, you have heard the male prisoner's story, what do you say to that ?

JACK. [*Turning to the* MAGISTRATE, *speaks suddenly in a confident, straightforward voice.*] The fact of the matter is, sir, that I'd been out to the theatre that

night, and had supper afterwards, and I came in
late.

MAGISTRATE. Do you remember this man being
outside when you came in?

JACK. No, sir. [*He hesitates.*] I don't think I do.

MAGISTRATE. [*Somewhat puzzled.*] Well, did he help
you to open the door, as he says? Did *any* one help
you to open the door?

JACK. No, sir—I don't think so, sir—I don't know.

MAGISTRATE. You don't know? But you must
know. It isn't a usual thing for you to have the
door opened for you, is it?

JACK. [*With a shamefaced smile.*] No.

MAGISTRATE. Very well, then——

JACK. [*Desperately.*] The fact of the matter is, sir,
I'm afraid I'd had too much champagne that night.

MAGISTRATE. [*Smiling.*] Oh! you'd had too much
champagne?

JONES. May I ask the gentleman a question?

MAGISTRATE. Yes—yes—you may ask him what
questions you like.

JONES. Don't you remember you said you was a
Liberal, same as your father, and you asked me wot
I was?

JACK. [*With his hand against his brow.*] I seem to
remember——

JONES. And I said to you, "I'm a bloomin' Con-
serva*tive*," I said; an' you said to me, "You look
more like one of these 'ere Socialists. Take wotever
you like," you said

JACK. [*With sudden resolution.*] No, I don't.   I don't remember anything of the sort.

JONES. Well, I do, an' my word's as good as yours. I've never been had up in a police court before. Look 'ere, don't you remember you had a sky-blue bag in your 'and——   [BARTHWICK *jumps.*

ROPER. I submit to your worship that these questions are hardly to the point, the prisoner having admitted that he himself does not remember anything. [*There is a smile on the face of Justice.*] It is a case of the blind leading the blind.

JONES. [*Violently.*] I've done no more than wot he 'as. I'm a poor man; I've got no money an' no friends—he's a toff—he can do wot I can't.

MAGISTRATE. Now, now! All this won't help you —you must be quiet. You say you took this box? Now, what made you take it? Were you pressed for money?

JONES. I'm always pressed for money.

MAGISTRATE. Was that the reason you took it?

JONES. No.

MAGISTRATE. [*To* SNOW.] Was anything found on him?

SNOW. Yes, your worship. There was six pounds twelve shillin's found on him, and this purse.

[*The red silk purse is handed to the* MAGIS-
    TRATE. BARTHWICK *rises in his seat, but
    hastily sits down again.*

MAGISTRATE. [*Staring at the purse.*] Yes, yes—let me see—— [*There is a silence.*] No, no, I've nothing before me as to the purse. How did you come by all that money?

JONES. [*After a long pause, suddenly.*] I declines to say.

MAGISTRATE. But if you had all that money, what made you take this box?

JONES. I took it out of spite.

MAGISTRATE. [*Hissing, with protruded neck.*] You took it out of spite? Well now, that's something ' But do you imagine you can go about the town taking things out of spite?

JONES. If you had my life, if you'd been out of work——

MAGISTRATE. Yes, yes; I know—because you're out of work you think it's an excuse for everything.

JONES. [*Pointing at* JACK.] You ask *'im* wot made *'im* take the——

ROPER. [*Quietly.*] Does your worship require this witness in the box any longer?

. MAGISTRATE. [*Ironically.*] I think not; he is hardly profitable.

> [JACK *leaves the witness-box, and, hanging his head, resumes his seat.*]

JONES. You ask 'im wot made 'im take the ady's——

> [*But the* BALD CONSTABLE *catches him by the sleeve.*]

BALD CONSTABLE. Sssh!

MAGISTRATE. [*Emphatically.*] Now listen to me

I've nothing to do with what he may or may not have taken. Why did you resist the police in the execution of their duty?

JONES. It warn't their duty to take my wife, a respectable woman, that 'adn't done nothing.

MAGISTRATE. But I say it was. What made you strike the officer a blow?

JONES. Any man would a struck 'im a blow. I'd strike 'im again, I would.

MAGISTRATE. You are not making your case any better by violence. How do you suppose we could get on if everybody behaved like you?

JONES. [*Leaning forward, earnestly.*] Well, wot about 'er; who's to make up to 'er for this? Who's to give 'er back 'er good name?

MRS. JONES. Your Worship, it's the children that's preying on his mind, because of course I've lost my work. And I've had to find another room owing to the scandal.

MAGISTRATE. Yes, yes, I know—but if he hadn't acted like this nobody would have suffered.

JONES. [*Glaring round at* JACK.] I've done no worse than wot 'e 'as. Wot I want to know is wot's goin' to be done to *'im*.

[*The* BALD CONSTABLE *again says " Hssh !"*

ROPER. Mr. Barthwick wishes it known, your Worship, that considering the poverty of the prisoners he does not press the charge as to the box. Perhaps your worship would deal with the case as one of disorder.

JONES. I don't want it smothered up, I want it all dealt with fair—I want my rights—

MAGISTRATE. [*Rapping his desk.*] Now you have said all you have to say, and you will be quiet.

> [*There is a silence ; the* MAGISTRATE *bends over and parleys with his* CLERK.

Yes, I think I may discharge the woman. [*In a kindly voice he addresses* MRS. JONES, *who stands unmoving with her hands crossed on the rail.*] It is very unfortunate for you that this man has behaved as he has. It is not the consequences to him but the consequences to you. You have been brought here twice, you have lost your work—[*He glares at* JONES] and this is what always happens. Now you may go away, and I am very sorry it was necessary to bring you here at all.

MRS. JONES. [*Softly.*] Thank you very much, your Worship.

> [*She leaves the dock, and looking back at* JONES, *twists her fingers and is still.*

MAGISTRATE. Yes, yes, but I can't pass it over. Go away, there's a good woman.

> [MRS. JONES *stands back. The* MAGISTRATE *leans his head on his hand: then raising it he speaks to* JONES.]

Now, listen to me. Do you wish the case to be settled here, or do you wish it to go before a Jury ?

JONES. [*Muttering.*] I don't want no Jury.

MAGISTRATE. Very well then, I will deal with it

here. [*After a pause.*] You have pleaded guilty to stealing this Box—

JONES. Not to stealin'—

BALD CONSTABLE. Hssshh

MAGISTRATE. And to assaulting the police——

JONES. Any man as was a man——

MAGISTRATE. Your conduct here has been most improper. You give the excuse that you were drunk when you stole the box. I tell you that is no excuse. If you choose to get drunk and break the law afterwards you must take the consequences. And let me tell you that men like you, who get drunk and give way to your spite or whatever it is that's in you, are—are—a *nuisance to the community.*

JACK. [*Leaning from his seat.*] Dad ' that's what you said to me ?

BARTHWICK. Tsst .

> [*There is a silence, while the* MAGISTRATE *consults his* CLERK ; JONES *leans forward waiting.*

MAGISTRATE. This is your first offence, and I am going to give you a light sentence. [*Speaking sharply, but without expression.*] One month with hard labour.

> [*He bends, and parleys with his* CLERK. *The* BALD CONSTABLE *and another help* JONES *from the dock.*

JONES. [*Stopping and twisting round.*] Call this justice ? What about 'im ? 'E got drunk ! 'E took

the purse—'e took the purse but [*in a muffled shout*]
it's *'is money got 'im* off—*Justice !*

> [*The prisoner's door is shut on* JONES, *and from
> the seedy-looking men and women comes a
> .hoarse and whispering groan.*

MAGISTRATE. We will now adjourn for lunch ! [*He
rises from his seat.*]

> [*The Court is in a stir.* ROPER *gets up and speaks
> to the reporter.* JACK, *throwing up his head,
> walks with a swagger to the corridor ;*
> BARTHWICK *follows.*

MRS. JONES. [*Turning to him with a humble gesture.*
Oh ! Sir !—

> [BARTHWICK *hesitates, then yielding to his
> nerves, he makes a shame-faced gesture of
> refusal, and hurries out of Court.* MRS.
> JONES *stands looking after him.*
>
> *The curtain falls.*

JOY

A PLAY ON THE LETTER "I
IN THREE ACTS

PERSONS OF THE PLAY

COLONEL HOPE, R.A., *retired*
MRS. HOPE, *his wife*
MISS BEECH, *their old governess*
LETTY, *their daughter*
ERNEST BLUNT, *her husband*
MRS. GWYN, *their niece*
JOY, *her daughter*
DICK MERTON, *their young friend*
HON. MAURICE LEVER. *their guest*
ROSE, *their parlourmaid*

TIME: The present. The action passes throughout midsummer day on the lawn of Colonel Hope's house, near the Thames above Oxford.

CAST OF THE ORIGINAL PRODUCTION
AT THE SAVOY THEATRE, LONDON,
ON SEPTEMBER 24, 1907

COLONEL HOPE	Mr. A. E. George
MRS. HOPE	Miss Henrietta Watson
MISS BEECH	Miss Florence Haydon
LETTY	Miss Mary Barton
ERNEST BLUNT	Mr. Frederick Lloyd
MRS. GWYN	Miss Wynne Matthison
JOY	Miss Dorothy Minto
DICK MERTON	Mr. Alan Wade
HON. MAURICE LEVER	Mr. Thalberg Corbet
ROSE	Miss Amy Lamborn

ACT I

[*The time is morning, and the scene a level lawn,
beyond which the river is running amongst fields. A
huge old beech tree overshadows everything, in the
darkness of whose hollow many things are hidden.
A rustic seat encircles it. A low wall clothed in
creepers, with two openings, divides this lawn from
the flowery approaches to the house. Close to the
wall there is a swing. The sky is clear and sunny.
COLONEL HOPE is seated in a garden-chair, reading
a newspaper through pince-nez. He is fifty-five,
and bald, with drooping grey moustaches and a
weather-darkened face. He wears a flannel suit,
and a hat from Panama ; a tennis racquet leans
against his chair. MRS. HOPE comes quickly through
the opening of the wall, with roses in her hands. She
is going grey; she wears tan gauntlets, and no hat.
Her manner is decided, her voice emphatic, as
though aware that there is no nonsense in its owner's
composition. Screened by the hollow tree, MISS
BEECH is seated ; and JOY is perched on a lower
branch, concealed by foliage.*

MRS. HOPE. I told Molly in my letter that she'd
have to walk up, Tom.

COLONEL. Walk up in this heat? My dear, why didn't you order Benson's fly?

MRS. HOPE. Expense for nothing ! Bob can bring up her things in the barrow. I've told Joy I won't have her going down to meet the train. She's so excited about her mother's coming there's no doing anything with her.

COLONEL. No wonder, after two months.

MRS. HOPE. Well, she's going home to-morrow she must just keep herself fresh for the dancing to-night. I'm not going to get people in to dance, and have Joy worn out before they begin.

COLONEL. [*Dropping his paper.*] I don't like Molly's walking up.

MRS. HOPE. A great strong woman like Molly Gwyn ! It isn't half a mile.

COLONEL. I don't like it, Nell; it's not hospitable.

MRS. HOPE. Rubbish ! If you want to throw away money, you must just find some better investment than those wretched three per cents of yours. The green-fly are in my roses already ! Did you ever see anything so *disgusting ?* [*They bend over the roses they have grown, and lose all sense of everything.*] Where's the syringe? I saw you mooning about with it last night, Tom.

COLONEL. [*Uneasily.*] Mooning ! [*He retires behind his paper. MRS. HOPE enters the hollow of the tree.*] There's an account of that West Australian swindle. Set of ruffians ! Listen to this, Nell ! " It is under-

stood that amongst the shareholders are large
numbers of women, clergymen, and Army officers."
How people can be such fools!

> [*Becoming aware that his absorption is unob-
> served, he drops his glasses, and reverses his
> chair towards the tree.*

MRS. HOPE. [*Reappearing with a garden syringe.*] I
simply won't have Dick keep his fishing things in the
tree; there's a whole potful of disgusting worms. *I*
can't touch them. *You* must go and take 'em out,
Tom. [*In his turn the* COLONEL *enters the hollow of the tree.*

MRS. HOPE. [*Personally.*] What on earth's the
pleasure of it? I can't see! He never catches anything worth eating.

> [*The* COLONEL *reappears with a paint pot full of
> worms; he holds them out abstractedly.*

MRS. HOPE. [*Jumping.*] Don't put them near me!

MISS BEECH. [*From behind the tree.*] Don't hurt the
poor creatures.

COLONEL. [*Turning.*] Hallo, Peachey? What are
you doing round there?

> [*He puts the worms down on the seat.*

MRS. HOPE. Tom, take the worms off that seat at
once!

COLONEL. [*Somewhat flurried.*] Good gad! *I* don't
know what to do with the beastly worms!

MRS. HOPE. It's not *my* business to look after
Dick's worms. Don't put them on the ground. I
won't have them anywhere where they can crawl
about.   [*She flicks some green fly off her roses.*

COLONEL. [*Looking into the pot as though the worms could tell him where to put them.*] Dash !

MISS BEECH. Give them to me.

MRS. HOPE. [*Relieved.*] Yes, give them to Peachey.

> [*There comes from round the tree* MISS BEECH,
> *old-fashioned, barrel-shaped, balloony in the
> skirts.   She takes the paint pot, and sits
> beside it on the rustic seat.*

MISS BEECH. Poor creatures !

MRS. HOPE. Well, it's beyond *me* how you can make pets of worms—wriggling, crawling, horrible things !

> [ROSE, *who is young and comely, in a pale print
> frock; comes from the house and places
> letters before her on a silver salver.*]

[*Taking the letters.*] What about Miss Joy's frock, Rose ?

ROSE. Please, 'm, I can't get on with the back without Miss Joy.

MRS. HOPE. Well, then you must just find her.   *I* don't know where she is.

ROSE. [*In a slow, sidelong manner.*] If you please, Mum, I think Miss Joy's up in the——

> [*She stops, seeing* MISS BEECH *signing to her with
> both hands.*

MRS. HOPE. [*Sharply.*] What is it, Peachey ?

MISS BEECH. [*Selecting a finger.*] Pricked meself !

MRS. HOPE. Let's look !

> [*She bends to look, but* MISS BEECH *places the
> finger in her mouth.*

Rose. [*Glancing askance at the* Colonel.] If you please, Mum, it's——below the waist, I think I can manage with the dummy.

Mrs. Hope. Well, you can try. [*Opening her letter as* Rose *retires*.] Here's Molly about her train.

Miss Beech. Is there a letter for me?

Mrs. Hope. No, Peachey.

Miss Beech. There never is.

Colonel. What's that? You got four by the first post.

Miss Beech. Exceptions!

Colonel. [*Looking over his glasses*.] Why! You know, you get 'em every day!

Mrs. Hope. Molly says she'll be down by the eleven thirty. [*In an injured voice*.] She'll be here in half an hour! [*Reading with disapproval from the letter*.] " Maurice Lever is coming down by the same train to see Mr. Henty about the Tocopala Gold Mine. Could you give him a bed for the night?"

                 [*Silence, slight but ominous.*

Colonel. [*Calling in to his aid his sacred hospitality*.] Of course we must give him a bed!

Mrs. Hope. Just like a man! What room I should like to know!

Colonel. Pink.

Mrs. Hope. As if *Molly* wouldn't have the Pink!

Colonel. [*Ruefully*.] I thought she'd have the blue!

Mrs. Hope. You know perfectly well it's full of earwigs, Tom. I killed ten there yesterday morning.

Miss Beech. Poor creatures!

Mrs. Hope. I don't know that I approve of this Mr. Lever's dancing attendance. Molly's only thirty-six.

Colonel. [*In a high voice.*] You can't refuse him a bed; I never heard of such a thing.

Mrs. Hope. [*Reading from the letter.*] " This gold mine seems to be a splendid chance. [*She glances at the* Colonel.] I've put all *my* spare cash into it. They're issuing some Preference shares now; if Uncle Tom wants an investment." [*She pauses, then in a changed, decided voice.*] Well, I suppose I shall have to screw him in somehow.

Colonel. What's that about gold mines? Gambling nonsense! Molly ought to know my views.

Mrs. Hope. [*Folding the letter away out of her consciousness.*] Oh! your views! This may be a specially good chance.

Miss Beech. Ahem! Special case!

Mrs. Hope. [*Paying no attention.*] I'm sick of these 3 per cent dividends. When you've only got so little money, to put it all into that India Stock, when it might be earning 6 per cent. at least, quite safely! There are ever so many things I want.

Colonel. There you go!

Mrs. Hope. As to Molly, *I* think it's high time her husband came home to look after her, instead of sticking out there in that hot place. In fact

[Miss Beech *looks up at the tree and exhibits cerebral excitement*]

I don't know what Geoff's about; why doesn't he

find something in England, where they could live together.

COLONEL. Don't say anything against Molly, Nell!

MRS. HOPE. Well, I don't believe in husband and wife being separated.   That's not my idea of married life.

[*The* COLONEL *whistles quizzically.*]
Ah, yes, she's *your* niece, not *mine!* Molly's very—

MISS BEECH. Ouch! [*She sucks her finger.*]

MRS. HOPE. Well, if I couldn't sew at your age, Peachey, without pricking my fingers! Tom, if I have Mr. Lever here, you'll just attend to what I say and look into that mine!

COLONEL. Look into your grandmother! I haven't made a study of geology for nothing. For every ounce you take out of a gold mine, you put an ounce and a half in.   Any fool knows that, eh, Peachey?

MISS BEECH. I hate your horrid mines, with all the poor creatures underground.

MRS. HOPE. Nonsense, Peachey! As if they'd go there if they didn't want to!

COLONEL. Why don't you read your paper, then you'd see what a lot of wild-cat things there are about.

MRS. HOPE. [*Abstractedly.*] I can't put Ernest and Letty in the blue-room, there's only the single bed. Suppose I put Mr. Lever there, and say nothing about the earwigs.   I daresay he'll never notice.

COLONEL. Treat a guest like that!

Mrs. Hope. Then where am I to put him for goodness sake ?

Colonel. Put him in my dressing-room, I'll turn out.

Mrs. Hope. Rubbish, Tom, I won't have you turned out, that's flat. He can have Joy's room, and she can sleep with the earwigs.

Joy. [*From her hiding-place upon a lower branch of the hollow tree.*] I won't.

[*Mrs. Hope and the Colonel jump.*

Colonel. God bless my soul !

Mrs. Hope. You wretched girl ? I told you never to climb that tree again. Did *you* know, Peachey ?

[*Miss Beech smiles.*]

She's always up there, spoiling all her frocks. Come down now, Joy; there's a good child !

Joy. I don't want to sleep with earwigs, Aunt Nell.

Miss Beech. *I'll* sleep with the poor creatures.

Mrs. Hope. [*After a pause.*] Well, it would be a mercy if you would for once, Peachey.

Colonel. Nonsense, I won't have Peachey——

Mrs. Hope. Well, who is to sleep there then ?

Joy. [*Coaxingly.*] Let me sleep with *Mother*, Aunt Nell, do !

Mrs. Hope. Litter her up with a great girl like you, as if we'd only one spare room ! Tom, see that she comes down—I can't stay here, I must manage something. [*She goes away towards the house.*

Colonel. [*Moving to the tree, and looking up.*] You heard what your Aunt said ?

Joy. [*Softly.*] Oh, Uncle Tom !

Colonel. I shall have to come up after you.

Joy. Oh, *do*, and Peachey too !

Colonel. [*Trying to restrain a smile.*] Peachey, you talk to her. [*Without waiting for* Miss Beech *however, he proceeds.*] What'll your Aunt say to me if I don't get you down ?

Miss Beech. Poor creature !

Joy. I don't want to be worried about my frock.

Colonel. [*Scratching his bald head.*] Well, *I* shall catch it.

Joy. Oh, Uncle Tom, your head is so beautiful from here ! [*Leaning over, she fans it with a leafy twig.*

Miss Beech. Disrespectful little toad !

Colonel. [*Quickly putting on his hat.*] You'll fall out, and a pretty mess that'll make on—[*he looks uneasily at the ground*]—*my* lawn !

> [*A voice is heard calling " Colonel ! Colonel !"*

Joy. There's Dick calling you, Uncle Tom.

> [*She disappears.*

Dick. [*Appearing in the opening of the wall.*] Ernie's waiting to play you that single, Colonel !

> [*He disappears.*

Joy. Quick, Uncle Tom ! Oh ! *do* go, before he finds I'm up here.

Miss Beech. Secret little creature !

> [*The* Colonel *picks up his racquet, shakes his fist, and goes away.*

Joy. [*Calmly.*] I'm coming down now, Peachey.

[*Climbing down.*] Look out! I'm dropping on your head.

Miss. Beech. [*Unmoved.*] Don't hurt yourself!

    [Joy *drops on the rustic seat and rubs her shin.*]
Told you so! [*She hunts in a little bag for plaster.*]
Let's see!

Joy. [*Seeing the worms.*] Ugh!

Miss Beech. What's the matter with the poor creatures?

Joy. They're so wriggly!

    [*She backs away and sits down in the swing.
She is just seventeen, light and slim, brown-
haired, fresh-coloured, and gray-eyed; her
white frock reaches to her ankles, she wears
a sun- bonnet.*]

Peachey, how long were you Mother's governess?

Miss Beech. Five years.

Joy. Was she as bad to teach as me?

Miss Beech. Worse!   [Joy *claps her hands.*]
She was the worst girl I ever taught.

Joy. Then you weren't fond of her?

Miss Beech. Oh! yes, I was.

Joy. Fonder than of me?

Miss Beech. Don't you ask such a lot of questions!

Joy. Peachey, duckie, what was Mother's *worst* fault?

Miss Beech. Doing what she knew she oughtn't.

Joy. Was she ever sorry?

Miss Beech. Yes, but she always went on doin' it.

Joy. *I* think being sorry's stupid !

Miss Beech.   Oh, do you ?

Joy. It isn't any good.   Was Mother revengeful, like me ?

Miss Beech. Ah ! Wasn't she ?

Joy. And jealous ?

Miss Beech. The most jealous girl I ever saw.

Joy. [*Nodding.*]   I *like* to be like her.

Miss Beech. [*Regarding her intently.*]   Yes ! you've got all your troubles before *you.*

Joy. Mother was married at eighteen, wasn't she, Peachey ?   Was she—was she much in love with Father then ?

Miss Beech. [*With a sniff.*]   About as much as usual.   [*She takes the paint pot, and walking round begins to release the worms.*

Joy. [*Indifferently.*]   They don't get on now, you know.

Miss Beech. What d'you mean by that, disrespectful little creature ?

Joy. [*In a hard voice.*] They haven't ever since *I've* known them.

Miss Beech. [*Looks at her, and turns away again.*] Don't talk about such things.

Joy. I suppose you don't know Mr. Lever ? [*Bitterly.*] He's such a cool beast.   He never loses his temper.

Miss Beech. Is that why you don't like him ?

Joy. [*Frowning.*] No—yes—I don't know.

Miss Beech. Oh ! perhaps you *do* like him ?

Joy. I don't; I hate him.

Miss Beech. [*Standing still.*] Fie! Naughty temper!

Joy. Well, so would you! He takes up all Mother's time.

Miss Beech. [*In a peculiar voice.*] Oh! does he?

Joy. When he comes *I* might just as well go to bed. [*Passionately.*] And now he's chosen to-day to come down here, when I haven't seen her for two months! Why couldn't he come when Mother and I'd gone home. It's simply brutal!

Miss Beech. But your mother likes him?

Joy. [*Sullenly.*] I don't *want* her to like him.

Miss Beech. [*With a long look at* Joy.] I see!

Joy. What are you doing, Peachey?

Miss Beech. [*Releasing a worm.*] Letting the poor creatures go.

Joy. If I tell Dick he'll never forgive you.

Miss Beech. [*Sidling behind the swing and plucking off* Joy's *sunbonnet. With devilry.*] Ah-h-h! You've done your hair up; so that's why you wouldn't come down!

Joy. [*Springing up, and pouting.*] I didn't want any one to see before Mother. You *are* a pig, Peachey!

Miss Beech. I thought there was *something!*

Joy. [*Twisting round.*] How does it look?

Miss Beech. I've seen better.

Joy. You tell any one before Mother comes, and see what I do!

MISS BEECH. Well, don't you tell about my worms, then!

JOY. Give me my hat! [*Backing hastily towards the tree, and putting her finger to her lips.*] Look out! Dick!

MISS BEECH. Oh! dear!

> [*She sits down on the swing, concealing the paint-pot with her feet and skirts.*

JOY. [*On the rustic seat, and in a violent whisper.*] I hope the worms will crawl up your legs!

> [DICK, *in flannels and a hard straw hat comes in. He is a quiet and cheerful boy of twenty. His eyes are always fixed on* JOY.

DICK. [*Grimacing.*] The Colonel's getting licked. Hallo! Peachey, in the swing?

JOY. [*Chuckling.*] Swing her, Dick!

MISS BEECH. [*Quivering with emotion.*] Little creature!

JOY. Swing her!   [DICK *takes the ropes.*

MISS BEECH. [*Quietly.*] It makes me sick, young man.

DICK. [*Patting her gently on the back.*] All right, Peachey.

MISS BEECH. [*Maliciously.*] Could you get me my sewing from the seat? Just behind Joy.

JOY. [*Leaning her head against the tree.*] If you do, I won't dance with you to-night.

> [DICK *stands paralysed.* MISS BEECH *gets off the swing, picks up the paint pot and stands concealing it behind her.*

Joy. Look what she's got behind *her*, sly old thing!

Miss Beech. Oh! dear!

Joy. Dance with her, Dick!

Miss Beech. If he dare!

Joy. Dance with her, or I won't dance with you to-night.   [*She whistles a waltz.*

Dick. [*Desperately.*] Come on then, Peachey. We *must*.

Joy. Dance, dance!

> [Dick *seizes* Miss Beech *by the waist. She drops the paint pot. They revolve.*

[*Convulsed.*] Oh, Peachey, oh!

> [Miss Beech *is dropped upon the rustic seat.*
> Dick *seizes* Joy's *hands and drags her up.*]

No, no! I won't!

Miss Beech. [*Panting.*] Dance, dance with the poor young man! [*She moves her hands.*] La la—la *la* la—la *la* la!   [Dick *and* Joy *dance.*

Dick. By Jove, Joy! You've done your hair up. I say, how jolly! You *do* look——

Joy. [*Throwing her hands up to her hair.*] I didn't mean *you* to see!

Dick. [*In a hurt voice.*] Oh! didn't you? I'm awfully sorry!

Joy. [*Flashing round.*] Oh, you old Peachey! [*She looks at the ground, and then again at* Dick.

Miss Beech. [*Sidling round the tree.*] Oh! dear!

Joy. [*Whispering.*] She's been letting out your worms.   [Miss Beech *disappears from view.*] Look!

DICK. [*Quickly.*] Hang the worms! Joy, promise *me* the second and fourth and sixth and eighth and tenth and supper, to-night. Promise! Do!

> [JOY *shakes her head.*]

It's not much to ask.

JOY. I won't promise anything.

DICK. Why not?

JOY. Because Mother's coming. I won't make any arrangements.

DICK. [*Tragically.*] It's our last night.

JOY. [*Scornfully.*] You don't understand! [*Dancing and clasping her hands.*] Mother's coming, mother's coming!

DICK. [*Violently.*] I wish—— Promise, Joy!

JOY. [*Looking over her shoulder.*] Sly old thing! If you'll pay Peachey out, I'll promise you supper!

MISS BEECH. [*From behind the tree.*] I hear you.

JOY. [*Whispering.*] Pay her out, pay her out! She's let out all your worms!

DICK. [*Looking moodily at the paint pot.*] I say, is it true that Maurice Lever's coming with your mother? I've met him playing cricket, he's rather a good sort.

JOY. [*Flashing out.*] *I* hate him.

DICK. [*Troubled.*] Do you? Why? I thought—I didn't know—if I'd *known* of course, I'd have——

> [*He is going to say "hated him too!" But the voices of* ERNEST BLUNT *and the* COLONEL *are heard approaching, in dispute.*]

Joy. Oh! Dick, hide me, I don't want my hair seen till Mother comes.

> [*She springs into the hollow tree. The* Colonel *and* Ernest *appear in the opening of the wall.*

Ernest. The ball *was* out, Colonel.

Colonel. Nothing of the sort.

Ernest. A good foot out.

Colonel. It was not, sir. I saw the chalk fly.

> [Ernest *is twenty-eight, with a little moustache, and the positive cool voice of a young man who knows that he knows everything. He is perfectly calm.*

Ernest. I was nearer to it than you.

Colonel. [*In a high, hot voice.*] I don't care where you were, I hate a fellow who can't keep cool.

Miss Beech. [*From behind the hollow tree.*] Fie! Fie!

Ernest. We're two to one, Letty says the ball was out.

Colonel. Letty's *your wife,* she'd say anything.

Ernest. Well, look here, Colonel, I'll show you the very place it pitched.

Colonel. Gammon! You've lost your temper, you don't know what you're talking about.

Ernest. [*Coolly.*] I suppose you'll admit the rule that one umpires one's own court.

Colonel. [*Hotly.*] Certainly not, *in this case!*

Miss Beech. [*From behind the hollow tree.*] Special case!

ERNEST. [*Moving chin in collar—very coolly.*] Well, of course if you won't play the game !

COLONEL. [*In a towering passion.*] If you lose your temper like this, I'll never play with you again.

> [*To* LETTY, *a pretty soul in a linen suit, approaching through the wall.*

Do you mean to say that ball was out, Letty ?

LETTY. Of course it was, father.

COLONEL. You say that because he's *your husband.* [*He sits on the rustic seat.*] If your mother 'd been there she'd have backed *me* up !

LETTY. Mother wants Joy, Dick, about her frock.

DICK. I—I don't know where she is.

MISS BEECH. [*From behind the hollow tree.*] Ahem !

LETTY. What's the matter, Peachey ?

MISS BEECH. Swallowed a fly.   Poor creature !

ERNEST. [*Returning to his point.*] Why I know the ball was out, Colonel, was because it pitched in a line with that arbutus tree——

COLONEL. [*Rising.*] Arbutus tree ! [*To his daughter.*] Where's your mother ?

LETTY. In the blue room, Father.

ERNEST. The ball was a good foot out; at the height it was coming when it passed me——

COLONEL. [*Staring at him.*] You're a—you're a—a theorist ! From where you were you couldn't see the ball at all.   [*To* LETTY.] Where's your mother ?

LETTY. [*Emphatically.*] In the *blue* room, Father !

> [*The* COLONEL *glares confusedly, and goes away towards the blue room.*

ERNEST. [*In the swing, and with a smile.*] Your old Dad'll never be a sportsman !

LETTY. [*Indignantly.*] I wish you wouldn't call Father old, Ernie ! What time's Molly coming, Peachey ?

> [ROSE *has come from the house, and stands waiting for a chance to speak.*

ERNEST. [*Breaking in.*] Your old Dad's only got one fault ; he can't take an *impersonal* view of things.

MISS BEECH. Can you find me any one who can ?

ERNEST. [*With a smile.*] Well, Peachey !

MISS BEECH. [*Ironically.*] Oh ! of course, there's you !

ERNEST. I don't know about that ! But——

ROSE. [*To* LETTY.] Please, Miss, the Missis says will you and Mr. Ernest please to move your things into Miss Peachey's room.

ERNEST. [*Vexed.*] Deuce of a nuisance havin' to turn out for this fellow Lever. What did Molly want to bring him for ?

MISS BEECH. Course you've no personal feeling in the matter !

ROSE. [*Speaking to* MISS BEECH.] The Missis says you're to please move your things into the blue room, please Miss.

LETTY. Aha, Peachey ! That settles you ! Come on, Ernie !

> [*She goes towards the house.* ERNEST, *rising from the swing, turns to* MISS BEECH, *who follows.*

ERNEST. [*Smiling, faintly superior.*] Personal, not a
bit ! I only think while Molly's out at grass, she
oughtn't to——

MISS BEECH. [*Sharply.*] Oh ! *do* you ?

> [*She hustles* ERNEST *out through the wall, but
> his voice is heard faintly from the distance :
> "*I *think it's jolly thin.*"

ROSE. [*To* DICK.] The Missis says you're to take all
your worms and things, Sir, and put them where
they won't be seen.

DICK. [*Shortly.*] Haven't got any !

ROSE. The Missis says she'll be very angry if you
don't put your worms away; and would you come and
help kill earwigs in the blue —— ?

DICK. Hang ! [*He goes, and* ROSE *is left alone.*

ROSE. [*Looking straight before her.*] Please, Miss Joy,
the Missis says will you go to her about your frock.

> [*There is a little pause, then from the hollow tree*
> JOY's *voice is heard.*

JOY. No—o !

ROSE. If you didn't come, I was to tell you she was
going to put you in the blue ——

> [JOY *looks out of the tree.*

[*Immovable, but smiling.*] Oh, Miss Joy, you've done
your hair up ! [JOY *retires into the tree.*
Please, Miss, what shall I tell the Missis ?

JOY. [JOY's *voice is heard.*] Anything you
like !

ROSE. [*Over her shoulder.*] I shall be drove to tell
her a story, Miss.

H

Joy. All right ! Tell it.

> [Rose *goes away, and* Joy *comes out.   She sits
> on the rustic seat and waits.*   Dick, *coming
> softly from the house, approaches her.*

Dick. [*Looking at her intently.*] Joy !   I wanted to
say something——

> [Joy *does not look at him, but twists her fingers.*]

I shan't see you again you know after to-morrow
till I come up for the 'Varsity match.

Joy. [*Smiling.*] But that's next week.

Dick. *Must* you go home to-morrow ?

> [Joy *nods three times.*]

[*Coming closer.*] I shall miss you so awfully.   You
don't know how I——   [Joy *shakes her head.*]
Do look at me ! [Joy *steals a look.*]   Oh ! Joy !

> [*Again* Joy *shakes her head.*

Joy. [*Suddenly.*] Don't !

Dick. [*Seizing her hand.*] Oh, Joy ! Can't you——

Joy. [*Drawing the hand away.*] Oh ! don't.

Dick. [*Bending his head.*] It's—it's—so——

Joy. [*Quietly.*] Don't, Dick !

Dick. But I can't help it ! It's too much for me,
Joy, I must tell you——

> [Mrs. Gwyn *is seen approaching towards the
> house.*

Joy. [*Spinning round.*] It's Mother—oh, *Mother !*

> [*She rushes at her.*

> [Mrs. Gwyn *is a handsome creature of thirty-six,
> dressed in a muslin frock.   She twists her
> daughter round, and kisses her.*

Mrs. Gwyn. How *sweet* you look with your hair up, Joy ! Who's this ? [*Glancing with a smile at* Dick.

Joy. Dick Merton—in my letters you know.

[*She looks at* Dick *as though she wished him gone.*

Mrs. Gwyn. How do you do ?

Dick. [*Shaking hands.*] How d'you do ? I think if you'll excuse me—I'll go in.

[*He goes uncertainly.*

Mrs. Gwyn. What's the matter with him ?

Joy. Oh, nothing ! [*Hugging her.*] Mother ! You *do* look such a duck. Why did you come by the towing-path, wasn't it *cooking* ?

Mrs. Gwyn. [*Avoiding her eyes.*] Mr. Lever wanted to go into Mr. Henty's.

[*Her manner is rather artificially composed.*

Joy. [*Dully.*] Oh ! Is he—is he really coming *here*, Mother ?

Mrs. Gwyn. [*Whose voice has hardened just a little.*] If Aunt Nell's got a room for him—of course—why not ?

Joy. [*Digging her chin into her mother's shoulder.*] Why couldn't he choose some day when we'd gone ? I wanted you all to myself.

Mrs. Gwyn. You *are* a quaint child—when I was your age——

Joy. [*Suddenly looking up.*] Oh ! Mother, you must have been a chook !

Mrs. Gwyn. Well, I was about twice as old as you, I know that.

Joy. Had you any—any other offers before you were married, Mother?

Mrs. Gwyn. [*Smilingly.*] Heaps!

Joy. [*Reflectively.*] Oh!

Mrs. Gwyn. Why? Have *you* been having any?

Joy. [*Glancing at* Mrs. Gwyn, *and then down.*] N—o, of course not!

Mrs. Gwyn. Where are they all? Where's Peachey?

Joy. Fussing about somewhere; don't let's hurry! Oh! you duckie—duckie! Aren't there any letters from Dad?

Mrs. Gwyn. [*In a harder voice.*] Yes, one or two.

Joy. [*Hesitating.*] Can't I see?

Mrs. Gwyn. I didn't bring them. [*Changing the subject obviously.*] Help me to tidy—I'm so hot I don't know what to do.

> [*She takes out a powder-puff bag, with a tiny looking-glass.*

Joy. How lovely it'll be to-morrow—going home!

Mrs. Gwyn. [*With an uneasy look.*] London's dreadfully stuffy, Joy. You'll only get knocked up again.

Joy. [*With consternation.*] Oh! but Mother, I *must* come.

Mrs. Gwyn. [*Forcing a smile.*] Oh, well if you must, you must!   [Joy *makes a dash at her.*] Don't rumple me again. Here's Uncle Tom.

Joy. [*Quickly.*] Mother, we're going to dance to-night, promise to dance with me, there are three

more girls than men, at least, and don't dance too
much with—with—you know—because I'm—[*dropping her voice and very still*]—jealous.

MRS. GWYN. [*Forcing a laugh.*]   You are funny!

JOY. [*Very quickly.*]   *I* haven't made any engage-
ments because of *you.*

[*The* COLONEL *approaches through the wall.*

MRS. GWYN. Well, Uncle Tom?

COLONEL. [*Genially.*]   Why, Molly!   [*He kisses
her.*]   What made you come by the towing-path?

JOY. Because it's so much cooler, of course.

COLONEL. Hallo!   What's the matter with *you?*
Phew! you've got your hair up!   Go and tell your
aunt your mother's on the lawn.   Cut along!

[*Joy goes, blowing a kiss.*]

Cracked about you, Molly!   Simply cracked!   We
shall miss her when you take her off to-morrow. [*He
places a chair for her.*]   Sit down, sit down, you must
be tired in this heat.   I've sent Bob for your things
with the wheelbarrow; what have you got—only a
bag, I suppose?

MRS. GWYN. [*Sitting, with a smile.*]   That's all,
Uncle Tom, except—my trunk and hat-box.

COLONEL. Phew!   And what's-his-name brought
a bag, I suppose?

MRS. GWYN. They're all together.   I hope it's
not too much, Uncle Tom.

COLONEL. [*Dubiously*]   Oh! Bob'll manage! I suppose you see a good deal of—of—Lever.   That's his
brother in the Guards, isn't it?

Mrs. Gwyn. Yes.

Colonel. Now what does this chap do?

Mrs. Gwyn. What should he do, Uncle Tom? He's a Director.

Colonel. Guinea-pig! [*Dubiously.*] Your bringing him down was a good idea.

> [Mrs. Gwyn, *looking at him sidelong, bites her lips.*]

I should like to have a look at him. But, I say, you know, Molly—mines, mines! There are a lot of these chaps about, whose business is to cook their own dinners. Your aunt thinks——

Mrs. Gwyn. Oh! Uncle Tom, don't tell me what Aunt Nell thinks!

Colonel. Well—well! Look here, old girl! It's *my* experience never to—what I mean is—never to trust too much to a man who has to do with mining. *I've* always refused to have anything to do with mines. If your husband were in England, of course, I'd say nothing.

Mrs. Gwyn. [*Very still.*] We'd better keep *him* out of the question, hadn't we?

Colonel. Of course, if you wish it, my dear.

Mrs. Gwyn. Unfortunately, I do.

Colonel. [*Nervously.*] Ah! yes, I know; but look here, Molly, your aunt thinks you're in a very delicate position—in fact, she thinks you see too much of young Lever——

Mrs. Gwyn. [*Stretching herself like an angry cat.*] Does she? And what do *you* think?

COLONEL. I ? I make a point of not thinking. I only know that here he is, and I don't want you to go burning your fingers, eh ?

[MRS. GWYN *sits with a vindictive smile.*] A gold mine's a *gold* mine. I don't mean he deliberately—but they take in women and parsons, and—and all sorts of fools. [*Looking down.*] And then, you know, I can't tell your feelings, my dear, and I don't want to ; but a man about town'll compromise a woman as soon as he'll look at her, and [*softly shaking his head.*] I don't like that, Molly ! It's not the thing !

> [MRS. GWYN *sits unmoved, smiling the same smile, and the* COLONEL *gives her a nervous look.*]

If—if you were any other woman—*I* shouldn't care —and if—if you were a plain woman, damme, you might do what you liked ! I know you and Geoff don't get on ; but here's this child of yours, devoted to you, and—and don't you see, old girl ? Eh ?

MRS. GWYN. [*With a little hard laugh.*] Thanks ! Perfectly ! I suppose as you don't think, Uncle Tom, it never occurred to you that *I* have rather a lonely time of it.

COLONEL. [*With compunction.*] Oh ! my dear, yes, of course I know it must be beastly.

MRS. GWYN. [*Stonily.*] It *is.*

COLONEL. Yes, yes ! [*Speaking in a surprised voice.*] I don't know what I'm talking like this for ! It's your Aunt ! She goes on at me till she gets on my

nerves. What d'you think she wants me to do now?
Put money into this gold mine! Did you ever hear
such folly?

MRS. GWYN. [*Breaking into laughter.*] Oh! Uncle
Tom!

COLONEL. All very well for you to laugh, Molly!

MRS. GWYN. [*Calmly.*] And how much *are* you
going to put in?

COLONEL. Not a farthing! Why, I've got nothing
but my pension and three thousand India Stock!

MRS. GWYN. Only ninety pounds a year, besides
your pension! D'you mean to say that's all you've
got, Uncle Tom? I never knew that before. What
a shame!

COLONEL. [*Feelingly.*] It *is*—a d--d shame! I don't
suppose there's another case in the army of a man
being treated as *I've* been.

MRS. GWYN. But how on earth do you manage
here on so little?

COLONEL. [*Brooding.*] Your Aunt's very funny.
She's a born manager. She'd manage the hind leg
off a donkey; but if *I* want five shillings for a charity
or what not, I have to whistle for it. And then all
of a sudden, Molly, she'll take it into her head to
spend goodness knows what on some trumpery or
other, and come to me for the money. If I haven't
got it to give her, out she flies about 3 per cent., and
worries me to invest in some wild-cat or other, like
your friend's thing, the Jaco—what is it? I don't
pay the slightest attention to her.

Mrs. Hope. [*From the direction of the house.*] Tom!

Colonel. [*Rising.*] Yes, dear! [*Then dropping his voice.*] I say, Molly, don't you mind what I said about young Lever. I don't wan't you to imagine that I think harm of people—you know I don't—but so many women come to grief, and—[*hotly*]—I can't stand men about town; not that he of course——

Mrs. Hope. [*Peremptorily.*] Tom!

Colonel. [*In hasty confidence.*] I find it best to let your Aunt run on. If she says anything——

Mrs. Hope. To-om!

Colonel. Yes, dear!

> [*He goes hastily.* Mrs. Gwyn *sits drawing circles on the ground with her charming parasol. Suddenly she springs to her feet, and stands waiting like an animal at bay.* The Colonel *and* Mrs. Hope *approach her talking.*

Mrs. Hope. Well, how was *I* to know?

Colonel. Didn't Joy come and tell you?

Mrs. Hope. I don't know what's the matter with that child? Well, Molly, so here you are. You're before your time—that train's always late.

Mrs. Gwyn. [*With faint irony.*] I'm sorry, Aunt Nell!

> [They *bob, seem to take fright, and kiss each other gingerly.*

Mrs. Hope. What have you done with Mr. Lever? I shall have to put him in Peachey's room. Tom's got no champagne.

COLONEL. They've a very decent brand down at the George, Molly, I'll send Bob over——

MRS. HOPE. Rubbish, Tom! He'll just have to put up with what he can get!

MRS. GWYN. Of course! He's not a snob! For goodness sake, Aunt Nell, don't put yourself out! I'm sorry I suggested his coming.

COLONEL. My dear, we *ought* to have champagne in the house—in case of accident.

MRS. GWYN. [*Shaking him gently by the coat.*] No, *please,* Uncle Tom!

MRS. HOPE. [*Suddenly.*] Now, I've told your Uncle, Molly, that he's not to go in for this gold mine without making certain it's a good thing. Mind, I think you've been very rash. I'm going to give you a good talking to; and that's not all—you oughtn't to go about like this with a young man; he's not at all bad looking. I remember him perfectly well at the Fleming's dance.

　　　[*On* MRS. GWYN'S *lips there comes a little mocking smile.*

COLONEL. [*Pulling his wife's sleeve.*] Nell!

MRS. HOPE. No, Tom, I'm going to talk to Molly; she's old enough to know better.

MRS. GWYN. Yes?

MRS. HOPE. Yes, and you'll get yourself into a mess; I don't approve of it, and when I see a thing I don't approve of——

COLONEL. [*Walking about, and pulling his moustache.*] Nell, I won't have it, I simply won't have it.

Mrs. Hope. What rate of interest are these Preference Shares to pay?

Mrs. Gwyn. [*Still smiling.*] Ten per cent.

Mrs. Hope. What did I tell you, Tom? And are they safe?

Mrs. Gwyn. You'd better ask Maurice.

Mrs. Hope. There, you see, you call him Maurice! Now supposing your Uncle went in for some of them——

Colonel. [*Taking off his hat—in a high, hot voice.*] I'm not going in for anything of the sort.

Mrs. Hope. Don't swing your hat by the brim! Go and look if you can see him coming!

[*The* Colonel *goes.*]

[*In a lower voice.*] Your Uncle's getting very bald. I've only shoulder of lamb for lunch, and a salad. It's lucky it's too hot to eat.

[Miss Beech *has appeared while she is speaking.*] Here she is, Peachey!

Miss Beech. I see her. [*She kisses* Mrs. Gwyn, *and looks at her intently.*]

Mrs. Gwyn. [*Shrugging her shoulders.*] Well, Peachey! What d'you make of me?

Colonel. [*Returning from his search.*] There's a white hat crossing the second stile. Is that your friend, Molly?

[Mrs. Gwyn *nods.*

Mrs. Hope. Oh! before I forget, Peachey—Letty and Ernest can move their things back again. I'm going to put Mr. Lever in *your* room. [*Catching sight*

of the paint pot on the ground.] There's that disgusting
paint-pot! Take it up at once, Tom, and put it in
the tree.

> [*The* COLONEL *picks up the pot and bears it to
> the hollow tree followed by* MRS. HOPE; *he
> enters.*

MRS. HOPE. [*Speaking into the tree.*] Not
there!

COLONEL. [*From within.*] Well, where then?

MRS. HOPE. Why—up—oh! gracious!

> [MRS. GWYN, *standing alone, is smiling.* LEVER
> *approaches from the towing-path. He is a
> man like a fencer's wrist, supple and steely.
> A man whose age is difficult to tell, with a
> quick, good-looking face, and a line between
> his brows; his darkish hair is flecked with
> grey. He gives the feeling that he has
> always had to spurt to keep pace with his
> own life.*

MRS. HOPE. [*Also entering the hollow tree.*] No—
oh!

COLONEL. [*From the depths, in a high voice.*] Well,
dash it then! What *do* you want?

MRS. GWYN. Peachey, may I introduce Mr. Lever
to you? Miss Beech, my old governess.

> [*They shake each other by the hand.*

LEVER. How do you do?

> [*His voice is pleasant, his manner easy.*

Miss Beech. Pleased to meet you.

> [*Her manner is that of one who is not pleased.*
> *She watches.*

Mrs. Gwyn. [*Pointing to the tree—maliciously.*] This
is my uncle and my aunt. They're taking exercise,
I think.

> [*The* Colonel *and* Mrs. Hope *emerge convul-*
> *sively.   They are very hot.*   Lever *and*
> Mrs. Gwyn *are very cool.*

Mrs. Hope. [*Shaking hands with him.*] So you've
got here !   Aren't you very hot ?—Tom !

Colonel. Brought a splendid day with you !
Splendid !

> [*As he speaks,* Joy *comes running with a bunch*
> *of roses ; seeing* Lever, *she stops and stands*
> *quite rigid.*

Miss Beech. [*Sitting in the swing.*] Thunder !

Colonel. Thunder ? Nonsense, Peachey, you're
always imagining something.   Look at the sky !

Miss Beech. Thunder !

> [Mrs. Gwyn's *smile has faded.*

Mrs. Hope. [*Turning.*] Joy, don't you see Mr.
Lever ?

> [Joy, *turning to her mother, gives her the roses.*
> *With a forced smile,* Lever *advances, holding*
> *out his hand.*

Lever. How are you, Joy?   Haven't seen you for
an age !

Joy. [*Without expression.*] I am very well, thank
you.

> [*She raises her hand, and just touches his.* MRS.
> GYWN'S *eyes are fixed on her daugher.* MISS
> BEECH *is watching them intently;* MRS. HOPE
> *is buttoning the* COLONEL'S *coat.*
>
> *The curtain falls.*

ACT II

[*It is afternoon, and at a garden-table placed beneath the hollow tree, the Colonel is poring over plans. Astride of a garden-chair,* LEVER *is smoking cigarettes. Dick is hanging Chinese lanterns to the hollow tree.*]

LEVER. Of course, if this level [*pointing with his cigarette*] peters out to the West we shall be in a tightish place; you know what a mine is at this stage, Colonel Hope.

COLONEL. [*Absently.*] Yes, yes. [*Tracing a line.*] What is there to prevent its running out here to the *East*?

LEVER. Well, nothing, except that as a matter of fact it doesn't.

COLONEL. [*With some excitement.*] I'm *very glad* you showed me these papers, very glad ! *I* say that its a most astonishing thing if the ore suddenly stops there.   [*A gleam of humour visits* LEVER'S *face.*] I'm not an expert, but you ought to prove that ground to the East more thoroughly.

LEVER. [*Quizzically.*] Of course, sir, if you advise that——

COLONEL. If it were *mine*, I'd no more sit down

under the belief that the ore stopped there; than I'd—— There's a harmony in these things.

LEVER. I can only tell you what our experts say.

COLONEL. Ah! Experts! No faith in them— never had! Miners, lawyers, theologians, cowardly lot—pays them to be cowardly. When they haven't their own axes to grind, they've got their theories; a theory's a dangerous thing. [*He loses himself in contemplation of the papers.*] Now *my* theory is, you're in strata here of what we call the Triassic Age.

LEVER. [*Smiling faintly.*] Ah!

COLONEL. You've struck a fault, that's what's happened. The ore may be as much as thirty or forty yards out; but it's there, depend on it.

LEVER. Would you back that opinion, Sir?

COLONEL. [*With dignity.*] I never give an opinion that I'm not prepared to back. I want to get to the *bottom* of this. What's to prevent the gold going down *indefinitely?*

LEVER. Nothing, so far as I know.

COLONEL. [*With suspicion.*] Eh!

LEVER. All I can tell you is: This is as far as we've got, and we want more money before we can get any further.

COLONEL. [*Absently.*] Yes, yes; that's very usual.

LEVER. If you ask my personal opinion I think it's very doubtful that the gold does go down.

COLONEL. [*Smiling.*] Oh! a *personal* opinion—on a matter of this sort!

LEVER. [*As though about to take the papers.*] Perhaps we'd better close the sitting, Sir; sorry to have bored you.

COLONEL. Now, now! Don't be so touchy! If I'm to put money in, I'm bound to look at it all round.

LEVER. [*With lifted brows.*] Please don't imagine that I *want* you to put money in.

COLONEL. Confound it, sir! D'you suppose I take you for a Company promoter?

LEVER. Thank you!

COLONEL. [*Looking at him doubtfully.*] You've got Irish blood in you—um? You're so hasty!

LEVER. If you're really thinking of taking shares —my advice to you is, don't!

COLONEL. [*Regretfully.*] If this were an ordinary gold mine, I wouldn't dream of looking at it, I want you to understand that. Nobody has a greater objection to gold mines than I.

LEVER. [*Looks down at his host with half-closed eyes.*] But it *is* a gold mine, Colonel Hope.

COLONEL. I know, I know; but I've been into it for *myself;* I've formed my *opinion personally.* Now, what's the reason you don't want me to invest?

LEVER. Well, if it doesn't turn out as you expect, you'll say it's my doing. I know what investors are.

COLONEL. [*Dubiously.*] If it were a Westralian or a Kaffir I wouldn't touch it with a pair of tongs! It's not as if I were going to put much in! [*He suddenly*

bends above the papers as though magnetically attracted.]
I like these Triassic formations !

> [DICK, *who has hung the last lantern, moodily
> departs.*

LEVER. [*Looking after him.*] That young man seems
depressed.

COLONEL. [*As though remembering his principles.*] I
don't like mines, never have ! [*Suddenly absorbed
again.*] I tell you what, Lever—this thing's got
tremendous possibilities. You don't seem to believe
in it enough. No mine's any good without faith ;
until I see for *myself*, however, I shan't commit myself beyond a thousand.

LEVER. Are you serious, sir ?

COLONEL. Certainly ! I've been thinking it over
ever since you told me Henty had fought shy. I've
a poor opinion of Henty. He's one of those fellows
that says one thing and does another. An oppor-
tunist !

LEVER. [*Slowly.*] I'm afraid we're all that, more or
less. [*He sits beneath the hollow tree.*

COLONEL. A man never knows what he is himself.
There's my wife. She thinks she's—— By the way,
don't say anything to her about this, please. And,
Lever [*nervously*], I don't think, you know, this is
quite the sort of thing for my niece.

LEVER. [*Quietly.*] I agree. I mean to get her out
of it.

COLONEL. [*A little taken aback.*] Ah ! You know,
she—she's in a very delicate position, living by her-

self in London. [LEVER *looks at him ironically*.] You [*very nervously*] see a good deal of her ? If it hadn't been for Joy growing so fast, we shouldn't have had the child down here. Her Mother ought to have her with her. Eh ! Don't you think so ?

LEVER. [*Forcing a smile*.] Mrs. Gwyn always seems to me to get on all right.

COLONEL. [*As though making a discovery*.] You know, I've found that when a woman's living alone and unprotected, the very least thing will set a lot of hags and jackanapes talking. [*Hotly*.] The more unprotected and helpless a woman is, the more they revel in it. If there's anything I hate in this world, it's those wretched creatures who babble about their neighbours' affairs.

LEVER. I agree with you.

COLONEL. One ought to be very careful not to give them—that is [*checks himself confused ; then hurrying on*]—I suppose you and Joy get on all right?

LEVER. [*Coolly*.] Pretty well, thanks. I'm not exactly in Joy's line ; haven't seen very much of her, in fact.

> [MISS BEECH *and* JOY *have been approaching from the house. But seeing* LEVER, JOY *turns abruptly, hesitates a moment, and with an angry gesture goes away.*

COLONEL [*Unconscious*.] Wonderfully affectionate little thing ! Well, she'll be going home to-morrow !

MISS BEECH. [*Who has been gazing after* JOY.] Talkin' business, poor creatures ?

LEVER. Oh, no! If you'll excuse me, I'll wash my hands before tea.

> [*He glances at the* COLONEL *poring over papers, and, shrugging his shoulders, strolls away.*

MISS BEECH. [*Sitting in the swing.*] I see your horrid papers.

COLONEL. Be quiet, Peachey!

MISS BEECH. On a beautiful summer's day, too.

COLONEL. That'll do now

MISS BEECH. [*Unmoved.*] For every ounce you take out of a gold mine you put two in.

COLONEL, Who told you that rubbish?

MISS BEECH. [*With devilry.*] *You did!*

COLONEL. This isn't an ordinary gold mine.

MISS BEECH. Oh! quite a *special* thing.

> [COLONEL *stares at her, but subsiding at her impassivity he pores again the over papers.*

> [ROSE *has approached with a tea cloth.*

ROSE. If you please, sir, the missis told me to lay the tea.

COLONEL. Go away! Ten fives fifty. Ten 5-16ths, Peachey?

MISS BEECH. I hate your nasty sums!

> [ROSE *goes away. The* COLONEL *writes.* MRS. HOPE'S *voice is heard,* "*Now then, bring those chairs, you two. Not that one, Ernest.*" ERNEST *and* LETTY *appear through the openings of the wall, each with a chair.*

COLONEL. [*With dull exasperation.*] What do *you* want !

LETTY. Tea, father.

                [*She places her chair and goes away.*

ERNEST. That Johnny-bird Lever is too cocksure for me, Colonel. Those South American things are no good at all. I know all about *them* from young Scrotton. There's not one that's worth a red cent. If you want a flutter——

COLONEL. [*Explosively.*] Flutter ! I'm not a gambler, sir !

ERNEST. Well, Colonel [*with a smile*], I only don't want you to chuck your money away on a stiff 'un. If you want anything good you should go to Mexico.

COLONEL. [*Jumping up and holding out the map.*] Go to—— [*He stops in time.*] What d'you call that, eh ? M-E-X——

ERNEST. [*Not to be embarrassed.*] It all depends on what part.

COLONEL. You think you know everything—you think nothing's right unless it's your own idea ! Be good enough to keep your advice to yourself.

ERNEST. [*Moving with his chair, and stopping with a smile.*] If you ask me, I should say it wasn't playing the game to put Molly into a thing like that.

COLONEL. What do you mean, sir ?

ERNEST. Any Juggins can see that she's a bit gone on our friend.

COLONEL. [*Freezingly.*] Indeed !

ERNEST. He's not at all the sort of Johnny that appeals to me.

COLONEL. Really?

ERNEST. [*Unmoved.*]   If I were you, Colonel, I should tip her the wink.   He was hanging about her at Ascot all the time.   It's a bit thick!

> [MRS. HOPE *followed by* ROSE *appears from the house.*

COLONEL. [*Stammering with passion.*]   Jackanapes!

MRS. HOPE. Don't stand there, Tom; clear those papers, and let Rose lay the table.   Now, Ernest, go and get another chair.

> [*The* COLONEL *looks wildly round and sits beneath the hollow tree, with his head held in his hands.   Rose lays the cloth.*

MISS BEECH. [*Sitting beside the* COLONEL.]   Poor creature!

ERNEST. [*Carrying his chair about with him.*]   Ask any Johnny in the City, he'll tell you Mexico's a very tricky country—the people are awful rotters—

MRS. HOPE. Put that chair down, Ernest.

> [ERNEST *looks at the chair, puts it down, opens his mouth, and goes away.   Rose follows him.*

What's he been talking about?   You oughtn't to get so excited, Tom; is your head bad, old man?   Here, take these papers!   [*She hands the papers to the* COLONEL.]   Peachey, go in and tell them tea'll be ready in a minute, there's a good soul!   Oh! and on my dressing-table you'll find a bottle of Eau de Cologne——

Miss Beech. Don't let him get in a temper again ? That's three times to-day !

> [*She goes towards the house.*

Colonel. Never met such a fellow in my life, the most opinionated, narrow-minded—thinks he knows everything. Whatever Letty could see in him I can't think. Pragmatical beggar !

Mrs. Hope. Now Tom ! What have you been up to, to get into a state like this ?

Colonel. [*Avoiding her eyes.*] I shall lose my temper with him one of these days. He's got that confounded habit of thinking nobody can be right but himself.

Mrs. Hope. That's enough ! I want to talk to you seriously ! Dick's in love. I'm perfectly certain of it.

Colonel. Love ! Who's he in love with— Peachey ?

Mrs. Hope. You can see it all over him. If I saw any signs of Joy's breaking out, I'd send them both away. I simply won't have it.

Colonel. Why, she's a child !

Mrs. Hope. [*Pursuing her own thoughts.*] But she isn't—not yet. I've been watching her very carefully. She's more in love with her Mother than any one, follows her about like a dog ! She's been quite rude to Mr. Lever.

Colonel. [*Pursuing his own thoughts.*] I don't believe a word of it.   [*He rises and walks about.*

Mrs. Hope. Don't believe a word of what ?

> [*The Colonel is silent.*]

[*Pursuing his thoughts with her own.*] If I thought
there were anything between Molly and Mr. Lever,
d'you suppose I'd have him in the house?

[THE COLONEL *stops, and gives a sort of grunt.*]
He's a very nice fellow; and I want you to pump
him well, Tom, and see what there is in this mine.

COLONEL. [*Uneasily.*] Pump!

MRS. HOPE. [*Looking at him curiously.*] Yes, you've
been up to something! Now what is it?

COLONEL. Pump my own guest! I never heard of
such a thing!

MRS. HOPE. There you are on your high horse! I
do wish you had a little common sense, Tom!

COLONEL. I'd as soon you asked me to sneak about
eavesdropping! Pump!

MRS. HOPE. Well, what were you looking at these
papers for? It does drive me so wild the way you
throw away all the chances you have of making a
little money. I've got you this opportunity, and you
do nothing but rave up and down, and talk nonsense!

COLONEL. [*In a high voice.*] Much you know about
it! I've taken a thousand shares in this mine!

[*He stops dead. There is a silence.*

MRS. HOPE. You've—WHAT? Without consulting
me? Well, then, you'll just go and take them out
again!

COLONEL. You want me to——?

MRS. HOPE. The idea! As if you could trust
your judgment in a thing like that! You'll just

go at once and say there was a mistake ; then we'll talk it over calmly.

COLONEL. [*Drawing himself up.*] Go back on what I've said ? Not if I lose every penny ! First you worry me to take the shares, and then you worry me not—I won't have it, Nell, I won't have it !

MRS. HOPE. Well, if I'd thought you'd have forgotten what you said this morning and turned about like this, d'you suppose I'd have spoken to you at all. Now, *do* you ?

COLONEL. Rubbish ! If you can't see that this is a special opportunity !

> [*He walks away followed by* MRS. HOPE, *who endeavours to make him see her point of view.* ERNEST *and* LETTY *are now returning from the house armed with a third chair.*

LETTY. What's the matter with everybody ? Is it the heat ?

ERNEST. [*Preoccupied and sitting in the swing.*] That sportsman, Lever, you know, ought to be warned off.

> [ROSE *has followed with the tea tray.*

LETTY. [*Signing to* ERNEST.] Where's Miss Joy, Rose ?

ROSE. Don't know, Miss.

> [*Putting down the tray, she goes.*

LETTY. Ernie, be careful, you never know where Joy is.

ERNEST. [*Preoccupied with his reflections.*] Your old Dad's as mad as a hatter with me.

LETTY. Why ?

ERNEST. Well, I merely said what I thought, that Molly ought to look out what she's doing, and he dropped on me like a cartload of bricks.

LETTY. The Dad's very fond of Molly.

ERNEST. But look here, d'you mean to tell me that she and Lever aren't——

LETTY. Don't! Suppose they are! If Joy were to hear it'd be simply awful. I *like* Molly. *I'm* not going to believe anything against her. I don't see the use of it. If it is, it is, and if it isn't, it isn't.

ERNEST. Well, all I know is that when I told her the mine was probably a frost she went for me like steam.

LETTY. Well, so should I. She was only sticking up for her friends.

ERNEST. Ask the old Peachey-bird. She knows a thing or two. Look here, I don't mind a man's being a bit of a sportsman, but I think Molly's bringin' him down here is too thick. Your old dad's got one of his notions that because this Josser's his guest, he must keep him in a glass case, and take shares in his mine, and all the rest of it.

LETTY. I do think people are horrible, always thinking things. It's not as if Molly were a stranger. She's *my own cousin*. I'm not going to believe anything about my own cousin. I simply *won't*.

ERNEST. [*Reluctantly realising the difference that this makes.*] I suppose it *does* make a difference, her bein' your cousin.

LETTY. Of course it does! I only hope to goodness no one will make Joy suspect——

> [*She stops and puts her finger to her lips, for*
> JOY *is coming towards them, as the tea-bell*
> *sounds. She is followed by* DICK *and* MISS
> BEECH *with the Eau de Cologne.* THE
> COLONEL *and* MRS. HOPE *are also coming*
> *back, discussing still each other's point of*
> *view.*

JOY. Where's Mother? Isn't she here?

MRS. HOPE. Now Joy, come and sit down; your mother's been told tea's ready; if she lets it get cold it's her look out.

DICK. [*Producing a rug, and spreading it beneath the tree.*] Plenty of room, Joy.

JOY. I don't believe Mother knows, Aunt Nell.

> [MRS. GWYN *and* LEVER *appear in the opening*
> *of the wall.*

LETTY. [*Touching* ERNEST's *arm.*] Look, Ernie! Four couples and Peachey——

ERNEST. [*Preoccupied.*] What couples?

JOY. Oh! Mums, here you are!

> [*Seizing her, she turns her back on* LEVER.
> *They sit in various seats, and* MRS. HOPE
> *pours out the tea.*

MRS. HOPE. Hand the sandwiches to Mr. Lever, Peachey. It's our own jam, Mr. Lever.

LEVER. Thanks. [*He takes a bite.*] It's splendid!

MRS. GWYN. [*With forced gaiety.*] It's the first time I've ever seen you eat jam.

LEVER. [*Smiling a forced smile.*] Really! But I love it.

MRS. GWYN. [*With a little bow.*] You always refuse mine.

JOY. [*Who has been staring at her enemy, suddenly.*] I'm all burnt up! Aren't you simply boiled, Mother?
[*She touches her Mother's forehead.*

MRS. GWYN. Ugh! You're quite clammy, Joy.

JOY. It's enough to make any one clammy.
[*Her eyes go back to LEVER's face as though to stab him.*

ERNEST. [*From the swing.*] I say, you know, the glass is going down.

LEVER. [*Suavely.*] The glass in the hall's steady enough.

ERNEST. Oh, I never go by that; that's a rotten old glass.

COLONEL. Oh! is it?

ERNEST. [*Paying no attention.*] I've got a little ripper—never puts you in the cart. Bet you what you like we have thunder before to-morrow night.

MISS BEECH. [*Removing her gaze from JOY to LEVER.*] You don't think we shall have it before to-night, do you?

LEVER. [*Suavely.*] I beg your pardon; did you speak to me?

MISS BEECH. I said, you don't think we shall have the thunder before to-night, do you?
[*She resumes her watch on JOY.*

LEVER. [*Blandly.*] Really, I don't see any signs of it.

> [JOY, *crossing to the rug, flings herself down.*
> *And* DICK *sits cross-legged, with his eyes*
> *fast fixed on her.*

MISS BEECH. [*Eating.*] People don't often see what they don't want to, do they?

> [LEVER *only lifts his brows.*

MRS. GWYN. [*Quickly breaking in.*] What *are* you talking about? The weather's perfect.

MISS BEECH. Isn't it.

MRS. HOPE. You'd better make a good tea, Peachey; nobody'll get anything till eight, and then only cold shoulder. You must just put up with no hot dinner, Mr. Lever.

LEVER. [*Bowing.*] Whatever is good enough for Miss Beech is good enough for me.

MISS BEECH. [*Sardonically—taking another sandwich.*] So you think!

MRS. GWYN. [*With forced gaiety.*] Don't be so absurd, Peachey.

> [MISS BEECH *grunts slightly.*

COLONEL. [*Once more busy with his papers.*] I see the name of your engineer is Rodriguez—Italian, eh?

LEVER. Portuguese.

COLONEL. Don't like that!

LEVER. I believe he was born in England.

COLONEL. [*Reassured.*] Oh, was he? Ah!

ERNEST. Awful rotters, those Portuguese!

COLONEL. There you go!

LETTY. Well, Father, Ernie only said what you said.

MRS. HOPE. Now I want to ask you, Mr. Lever, is this gold mine safe? If it isn't—I simply won't allow Tom to take these shares; he can't afford it.

LEVER. It rather depends on what you call safe, Mrs. Hope.

MRS. HOPE. I don't want anything extravagant, of course; if they're going to pay their 10 per cent. regularly, and Tom can have his money out at any time—— [*There is a faint whistle from the swing.*] I only want to know that it's a thoroughly genuine thing.

MRS. GWYN. [*Indignantly.*] As if Maurice would be a director if it wasn't?

MRS. HOPE. Now Molly, I'm simply asking——

MRS. GWYN. Yes, you are!

COLONEL. [*Rising.*] I'll take two thousand of those shares, Lever. To have my wife talk like that—I'm quite ashamed.

LEVER. Oh, come, sir, Mrs. Hope only meant——
[MRS. GWYN *looks eagerly at* LEVER.

DICK. [*Quietly.*] Let's go on the river, Joy.
[JOY *rises, and goes to her Mother's chair.*

MRS. HOPE. Of course! What rubbish, Tom! As if any one ever invested money without making sure!

LEVER. [*Ironically.*] It seems a little difficult to make sure in this case. There isn't the smallest necessity for Colonel Hope to take any shares, and it looks to me as if he'd better not.

[He lights a cigarette.

MRS. HOPE. Now, Mr. Lever, don't be offended! I'm very anxious for Tom to take the shares if you say the thing's so good.

LEVER. I'm afraid I must ask to be left out, please.

JOY. *[Whispering.]* Mother, if you've finished, do come, I want to show you my room.

MRS. HOPE. I wouldn't say a word, only Tom's so easily taken in.

MRS. GWYN. *[Fiercely.]* Aunt Nell, how *can* you?

*[*JOY *gives a little savage laugh.*

LETTY. *[Hastily.]* Ernie, will you play Dick and me? Come on, Dick!   *[All three go out towards the lawn.*

MRS. HOPE. You ought to know your Uncle by this time, Molly. He's just like a child. He'd be a pauper to-morrow if I didn't see to things.

COLONEL. Understand once for all that I shall take two thousand shares in this mine. I'm—I'm humiliated.   *[He turns and goes towards the house.*

MRS. HOPE. Well, what on earth have I said?

[She hurries after him.

MRS. GWYN. *[In a low voice as she passes.]* You needn't insult my friends!

     *[*LEVER, *shrugging his shoulders, has strolled aside.* JOY, *with a passionate movement seen only by* MISS BEECH, *goes off towards the house.* MISS BEECH *and* MRS. GWYN *are left alone beside the remnants of the feast.*

Miss Beech. Molly ! [Mrs. Gwyn *looks up startled.*]
Take care, Molly, take care ! The child ! Can't
you see ? [*Apostrophizing* Lever.] Take care, Molly,
take care !

Lever. [*Coming back.*] Awfully hot, isn't it ?

Miss Beech. Ah ! and it'll be hotter if we don't
mind.

Lever. [*Suavely.*] Do we control these things ?

> [Miss Beech *looking from face to face, nods her*
> *head repeatedly ; then gathering her skirts*
> *she walks towards the house.* Mrs. Gwyn
> *sits motionless, staring before her.*]

Extraordinary old lady ! [*He pitches away his cigar-*
ette.] What's the matter with her, Molly ?

Mrs. Gwyn. [*With an effort.*] Oh ! Peachey's a
character !

Lever. [*Frowning.*] So I see ! [*There is a silence.*
Mrs. Gwyn. Maurice !

Lever. Yes.

Mrs. Gywn. Aunt Nell's hopeless, you mustn't
mind her.

Lever. [*In a dubious and ironic voice.*] My dear girl,
I've too much to bother me to mind trifles like
that.

Mrs. Gwyn. [*Going to him suddenly.*] Tell *me*, won't
you ? [Lever *shrugs his shoulders.*]
A month ago you'd have told me soon enough !

Lever. Now, Molly !

Mrs. Gwyn. Ah ! [*With a bitter smile.*] The Spring's
soon over.

LEVER. It's always Spring between us.

MRS. GWYN. Is it?

LEVER. You didn't tell me what *you* were thinking about just now when you sat there like stone.

MRS. GWYN. It doesn't do for a *woman* to say too much.

LEVER. Have I been so bad to you that you need feel like that, Molly?

MRS. GWYN. [*With a little warm squeeze of his arm.*] Oh! my *dear*, it's only that I'm so ———   [*She stops.*

LEVER. [*Gently*]. So what?

MRS. GWYN. [*In a low voice.*] It's hateful here.

LEVER. I didn't want to come. I don't understand why you suggested it. [MRS. GYWN *is silent.*] It's been a mistake!

MRS. GWYN. [*Her eyes fixed on the ground.*] Joy comes *home* to-morrow. I thought if I brought you here—I should know——

LEVER. [*Vexedly.*] Um!

MRS. GWYN. [*Losing her control.*] Can't you *see*? It haunts me? How are we to go on? I must know—I must know!

LEVER. I don't see that my coming——

MRS. GWYN. I thought I should have more confidence; I thought I should be able to face it better in London, if you came down here openly—and now —I feel I mustn't speak or look at you.

LEVER. You don't think your Aunt——

MRS. GWYN. [*Scornfully.*] She! It's only Joy I care about.

LEVER. [*Frowning.*] We must be more careful, that's all. We mustn't give ourselves away again, as we were doing just now.

MRS. GWYN. When any one says anything horrid to you, I can't help it.

> [*She puts her hand on the lappel of his coat.*

LEVER. My dear child, take care!

> [MRS. GWYN *drops her hand. She throws her head back, and her throat is seen to work as though she were gulping down a bitter draught. She moves away.*]

[*Following hastily.*] Don't dear, don't! I only meant —— Come, Molly, let's be sensible. I want to tell you something about the mine.

MRS. GWYN. [*With a quavering smile.*] Yes—let's talk sensibly, and walk properly in this sensible, proper place.

> [LEVER *is seen trying to soothe her, and yet to walk properly. As they disappear, they are viewed by* JOY, *who like the shadow parted from its figure, has come to join it again. She stands now, foiled, a carnation in her hand; then flings herself on a chair, and leans her elbows on the table.*

JOY. I hate him! Pig!

ROSE. [*Who has come to clear the tea things.*] Did you call, Miss

JOY. Not you!

ROSE. [*Motionless.*] No, Miss!

Joy. [*Leaning back and tearing the flow er.*] Oh! do hurry up, Rose!

Rose. [*Collects the tea things.*] Mr. Dick's coming down the path! Aren't I going to get you to do your frock, Miss Joy?

Joy. No.

Rose. What will the Missis say?

Joy. Oh, *don't* be so stuck, Rose!

[Rose *goes, but* Dick *has come.*

Dick. Come on the river, Joy, just for half an hour, as far as the kingfishers—do! [Joy *shakes her head.*] Why not? It'll be so jolly and cool. I'm most awfully sorry if I worried you this morning. I didn't mean to. I won't again, I promise. [Joy *slides a look at him, and from that look he gains a little courage.*] *Do* come! It'll be the last time. *I* feel it awfully, Joy.

Joy. There's nothing to hurt *you!*

Dick. [*Gloomily.*] Isn't there—when you're like this?

Joy. [*In a hard voice.*] If you don't like me, why do you follow me about?

Dick. What *is* the matter?

Joy. [*Looking up, as if for want of air.*] Oh! Don't!

Dick. Oh, Joy, what *is* the matter? Is it the heat?

Joy. [*With a little laugh.*] Yes.

Dick. Have some Eau de Cologne. I'll make you a bandage. [*He takes the Eau de Cologne, and makes a bandage with his handkerchief.*] It's *quite* clean.

JOY. Oh, Dick, you are so funny!

DICK. [*Bandaging her forehead.*] I can't bear *you* to feel bad; it puts me off completely. I mean I don't generally make a fuss about people, but when it's *you*——

JOY. [*Suddenly.*] I'm all right.

DICK. Is that comfy?

JOY. [*With her chin up, and her eyes fast closed.*] Quite.

DICK. I'm not going to stay and worry you. You ought to rest. Only, Joy! Look here! If you want me to do *anything* for you, *any* time——

JOY. [*Half opening her eyes.*] Only to go away.

[DICK *bites his lips and walks away.*

Dick—[*softly*]—Dick! [DICK *stops.*] I didn't mean that; will you get me some water-irises for this evening?

DICK. Won't I? [*He goes to the hollow tree and from its darkness takes a bucket and a boat-hook.*] I know where there are some rippers!

[JOY *stays unmoving with her eyes half closed.*] Are you sure you're all right, Joy? You'll just rest here in the shade, won't you, till I come back; it'll do you no end of good. I shan't be twenty minutes.

[*He goes, but cannot help returning softly, to make sure.*]

You're *quite* sure you're all right?

[JOY *nods. He goes away towards the river. But there is no rest for* JOY. *The voices of* MRS. GWYN *and* LEVER *are heard returning.*

Joy. [*With a gesture of anger.*] Hateful! Hateful!
[*She runs away.*

[Mrs. Gwyn *and* Lever *are seen approaching;
they pass the tree, in conversation.*

Mrs. Gwyn. But I don't see why, Maurice.

Lever. We mean to sell the mine; we must do
some more work on it, and for that we must have
money.

Mrs. Gwyn. If you only want a little, I should
have thought you could have got it in a minute in
the City.

Lever. [*Shaking his head.*] No, no; we must get it
privately.

Mrs. Gwyn. [*Doubtfully.*] Oh! [*She slowly adds.*]
Then it isn't such a good thing!

[*And she does not look at him.*

Lever. Well, we mean to sell it.

Mrs. Gwyn. What about the people who buy?

Lever. [*Dubiously regarding her.*] My dear girl,
they've just as much chance as *we* had. It's not my
business to think of them. There's *your* thousand
pounds——

Mrs. Gwyn. [*Softly.*] Don't bother about *my*
money, Maurice. I don't want you to do anything
not quite——

Lever. [*Evasively.*] Oh! There's my brother's
and my sister's too. I'm not going to let any of you
run any risk. When we all went in for it the thing
looked splendid; it's only the last month that we've
had doubts. What bothers me now is your Uncle.

I don't want him to take these shares. It looks as if I'd come here on purpose.

MRS. GWYN. Oh! he *mustn't* take them!

LEVER. That's all very well; but it's not so simple.

MRS. GWYN. [*Shyly.*] But, Maurice, have you told him about the selling?

LEVER. [*Gloomily, under the hollow tree.*] It's a Board secret. I'd no business to tell even you.

MRS. GWYN. But he thinks he's taking shares in a good—a permanent thing.

LEVER. You can't go into a mining venture without some risk.

MRS. GWYN. Oh, yes, I know—but—but Uncle Tom is such a dear!

LEVER. [*Stubbornly.*] I can't help his being the sort of man he is. I didn't want him to take these shares, I told him so in so many words. Put yourself in my place, Molly, how can I go to him and say—" This thing may turn out rotten," when he knows I got you to put your money into it?

> [*But* JOY, *the lost shadow, has come back. She moves forward resolutely. They are divided from her by the hollow tree; she is unseen. She stops.*]

MRS. GWYN. I think he *ought* to be told about the selling; it's not fair.

LEVER. What on earth made him rush at the thing like that? I don't understand that kind of man?

Mrs. Gwyn. [*Impulsively.*] I *must* tell him, Maurice;
I can't let him take the shares without——

> [*She puts her hand on his arm.*
> [Joy *turns, as if to go back whence she came, but
> stops once more.*

Lever. [*Slowly and very quietly.*] I didn't think
you'd give *me* away, Molly.

Mrs. Gwyn. I don't think I quite understand.

Lever. If you tell the Colonel about this sale
the poor old chap will think me a man that you
ought to have nothing to do with. Do you want
that ?

> [Mrs. Gwyn, *giving her lover a long look,
> touches his sleeve.* Joy, *slipping behind the
> hollow tree, has gone.*]

You can't act in a case like this as if you'd only a
principle to consider. It's the—the *special circumstances*——

Mrs. Gwyn. [*With a faint smile.*] But you'll be
glad to get the money, won't you ?

Lever. By George, if you're going to take it like
this, Molly !

Mrs. Gwyn. Don't !

Lever. We may not sell after all, dear, we may
find it turn out trumps.

Mrs. Gwyn. [*With a shiver.*] I don't want to hear
any more. I know women don't understand. [*Impulsively.*] It's only that I can't bear any one should
think that *you*——

Lever. [*Distressed.*] For goodness' sake, don't look

like that, Molly! Of course, I'll speak to your
Uncle. I'll stop him somehow, even if I have to
make a fool of myself. I'll do anything you
want——

MRS. GWYN. I feel as if I were being smothered
here.

LEVER. It's only for one day.

MRS. GWYN. [*With sudden tenderness.*] It's not your
fault, dear. I ought to have known how it would be.
Well, let's go in !

> [*She sets her lips, and walks towards the house
> with* LEVER *following. But no sooner has
> she disappeared than* JOY *comes running
> after ; she stops, as though throwing down a
> challenge. Her cheeks and ears are burning.*

JOY. Mother!

> [*After a moment* MRS. GWYN *reappears in the
> opening of the wall.*

MRS. GWYN. Oh! here you are !

JOY. [*Breathlessly.*] Yes.

MRS. GWYN. [*Uncertainly.*] Where—have you been?
You look dreadfully hot; have you been running ?

JOY. Yes—no.

MRS. GWYN. [*Looking at her fixedly.*] What's the
matter—you're trembling ! [*Softly.*] Aren't you well,
dear ?

JOY. Yes—I don't know.

MRS. GWYN. What *is* it, darling ?

JOY. [*Suddenly clinging to her.*] Oh ! Mother !

MRS. GWYN. I don't understand.

Joy. [*Breathlessly.*] Oh, Mother, let me go back home with you now at once——

Mrs. Gwyn. [*Her face hardening.*] Why? What on earth——

Joy. I can't stay here.

Mrs. Gwyn. But why?

Joy. I want to be with *you*—Oh! Mother, don't you love me?

Mrs. Gwyn. [*With a faint smile.*] Of course I love you, Joy.

Joy. Ah! but you love *him* more.

Mrs. Gwyn. Love him—whom?

Joy. Oh! Mother, I didn't——[*She tries to take her Mother's hand, but fails.*] Oh! don't.

Mrs. Gwyn. You'd better explain what you mean, I think.

Joy. I want to get you to—he—he's—he's—not——!

Mrs. Gwyn. [*Frigidly.*] Really, Joy!

Joy. [*Passionately.*] I'll fight against him, and I know there's something wrong about——

[*She stops.*

Mrs. Gwyn. About what?

Joy. Let's tell Uncle Tom, Mother, and go away.

Mrs. Gwyn. Tell Uncle Tom—what?

Joy. [*Looking down and almost whispering.*] About—about—the mine.

Mrs. Gwyn. What about the mine? What do you mean? [*Fiercely.*] Have you been spying on me?

Joy. [*Shrinking.*] No! oh, no!

Mrs. Gwyn. Where were you?

Joy. [*Just above her breath.*] I—I heard something.

Mrs. Gwyn. [*Bitterly.*] But you were not spying?

Joy. I wasn't—I wasn't! I didn't want—to hear. I only heard a little. I couldn't help listening, Mother.

Mrs. Gwyn. [*With a little laugh.*] Couldn't help listening?

Joy. [*Through her teeth.*] I *hate him*. I didn't mean to listen, but I hate him.

Mrs. Gwyn. I see. [*There is a silence.*] Why do you hate him?

Joy. He—he—— [*She stops.*

Mrs. Gwyn. Yes?

Joy. [*With a sort of despair.*] I don't know. Oh! I *don't know!* But I feel——

Mrs. Gwyn. I can't reason with you. As to what you heard, it's—ridiculous.

Joy. It's not that. It's—it's you!

Mrs. Gwyn. [*Stonily.*] I don't know what you mean.

Joy. [*Passionately.*] I wish Dad were here!

Mrs. Gwyn. Do you love your Father as much as me?

Joy. Oh! Mother, no—you *know* I don't.

Mrs. Gwyn. [*Resentfully.*] Then why do you want him?

Joy. [*Almost under her breath.*] Because of that man.

Mrs. Gwyn. Indeed!

Joy. I will never—never make friends with him.

Mrs. Gwyn. [*Cuttingly.*] I have not asked you to.

Joy. [*With a blind movement of her hand.*] Oh, Mother!

[Mrs. Gwyn *half turns away.*]

Mother—won't you? Let's tell Uncle Tom, and go away from him?

Mrs. Gwyn. If you were not a child, Joy, you wouldn't say such things.

Joy. [*Eagerly.*] I'm not a child, I'm—I'm a woman. I *am*.

Mrs. Gwyn. No! You—are—*not* a woman, Joy.

[*She sees* Joy *throw up her arms as though warding off a blow, and turning finds that* Lever *is standing in the opening of the wall.*

Lever. [*Looking from face to face.*] What's the matter? [*There is no answer.*] What is it, Joy?

Joy. [*Passionately.*] I heard you, I don't care who knows. I'd listen again.

Lever. [*Impassively.*] Ah! and what did I say that was so very dreadful?

Joy. You're a—a—you're a—coward!

Mrs. Gwyn. [*With a sort of groan.*] Joy!

Lever. [*Stepping up to* Joy, *and standing with his hands behind him—in a low voice.*] Now, hit me in the face—hit me—hit me as hard as you can. Go on, Joy, it'll do you good.

[Joy *raises her clenched hand, but drops it, and hides her face.*]

Why don't you ?   I'm not pretending !

> [Joy *makes no sign.*]

Come Joy; you'll make yourself ill, and that won't help, will it ?

> [*But* Joy *still makes no sign.*]

[*With determination.*]   What's the matter; now come—tell me !

Joy. [*In a stifled, sullen voice.*]   Will you leave my mother alone ?

Mrs. Gwyn.   Oh ! my dear Joy, don't be silly !

Joy. [*Wincing; then with sudden passion.*]   I defy you—I defy you !

> [*She rushes from their sight.*

Mrs. Gwyn. ⌊*With a movement of distress.*]   Oh !

Lever.   [*Turning to* Mrs. Gwyn *with a protecting gesture.*]   Never mind, dear !   It'll be—it'll be all right !

> [*But the expression of his face is not the expression of his words.*
>
> *The curtain falls.*

ACT III

[*It is evening; a full yellow moon is shining through
the branches of the hollow tree. The Chinese
lanterns are alight. There is dancing in the house;
the music sounds now loud, now soft. Miss Beech
is sitting on the rustic seat in a black bunchy evening
dress, whose inconspicuous opening is inlaid with
white. She slowly fans herself.*

[Dick *comes from the house in evening dress. He does
not see* Miss Beech.

Dick. Curse ! [*A short silence.*] Curse !

Miss Beech. Poor young man !

Dick. [*With a start.*] Well, Peachey, I can't help it.
[*He fumbles off his gloves.*

Miss Beech. Did you ever know any one that
could ?

Dick. [*Earnestly.*] It's such awfully hard lines on
Joy. I can't get her out of my head, lying there
with that beastly headache while everybody's jigging
round.

Miss Beech. Oh ! you don't mind about yourself
—noble young man !

Dick. I should be a brute if I didn't mind more
for her.

Miss Beech. So you think it's a headache, do you?

Dick. Didn't you hear what Mrs. Gwyn said at dinner about the sun? [*With inspiration.*] I say, Peachey, couldn't you—couldn't you just go up and give her a message from me, and find out if there's anything she wants, and say how brutal it is that she's seedy; it would be most awfully decent of you. And tell her the dancing's no good without her. Do, Peachey, now do! Ah! and look here!

> [*He dives into the hollow of the tree, and brings from out of it a pail of water, in which are placed two bottles of champagne, and some yellow irises—he takes the irises.*]

You might give her these. I got them specially for her, and I haven't had a chance.

Miss Beech. [*Lifting a bottle.*] What's this?

Dick. Fizz. The Colonel brought it from the George. It's for supper; he put it in here because of—— [*Smiling faintly*] Mrs. Hope, I think. Peachey, *do* take her those irises.

Miss Beech. D'you think they'll do her any good?

Dick. [*Crestfallen.*] I thought she'd like—— I don't want to worry her—you might try.

> [Miss Beech *shakes her head.*]

Why not?

Miss Beech. The poor little creature won't let me in.

Dick. You've *been* up then!

Miss Beech. [*Sharply.*] Of course I've been up. I've not got a stone for my heart, young man!

DICK. All right ! I suppose I shall just have to get along somehow.

MISS BEECH. [*With devilry.*] That's what we've all got to do.

DICK. [*Gloomily.*] But this is too brutal for anything !

MISS BEECH. Worse than ever happened to any one !

DICK. I swear I'm not thinking of *myself*.

MISS BEECH. Did y'ever know anybody that swore they were ?

DICK. Oh ! shut up !

MISS BEECH. You'd better go in and get yourself a partner.

DICK. [*With pale desperation.*] Look here, Peachey, I simply loathe all those girls.

MISS BEECH. Ah—h ! [*Ironically.*] Poor lot, aren't they ?

DICK. All right ; chaff away, it's good fun, isn't it ? It makes me sick to dance when Joy's lying there. Her last night, too !

MISS BEECH. [*Sidling to him.*] You're a good young man, and you've got a good heart.

[*She takes his hand, and puts it to her cheek.*

DICK. Peachey—I say Peachey — d'you think there's—I mean d'you think there'll ever be any chance for me ?

MISS BEECH. I *thought* that was coming ! I don't approve of your making love at your time of life ; don't you think I'm going to encourage you.

DICK. But I shall be of age in a year; my money's my own, it's not as if I had to ask any one's leave; and I mean, I *do* know my own mind.

MISS BEECH. Of course you do. Nobody else would at your age, but *you* do.

DICK. I wouldn't ask her to promise, it wouldn't be fair when she's so young, but I do want her to know that I shall never change.

MISS BEECH. And suppose—only suppose—she's fond of you, and says *she'll* never change.

DICK. Oh! Peachey! D'you think there's a chance of that—*do* you?

MISS BEECH. A—h—h!

DICK. I wouldn't let her bind herself, I swear I wouldn't. [*Solemnly.*] I'm not such a selfish brute as you seem to think.

MISS BEECH. [*Sidling close to him and in a violent whisper.*] Well—*have a go !*

DICK. Really? You *are* a brick, Peachey!

[*He kisses her.*

MISS BEECH. [*Yielding pleasurably; then remembering her principles.*] Don't you ever say I said so! You're too young, both of you.

DICK. But it is exceptional, I mean in *my* case, isn't it?

[*The Colonel and* MRS. GWYN *are coming down the lawn.*

MISS BEECH. Oh! *very !*

[*She sits beneath the tree and fans herself.*

COLONEL. The girls are all sitting out, Dick ! I've been obliged to dance myself. Phew !

> [*He mops his brow.*]
>> [DICK *swinging round goes rushing off towards the house.*]

[*Looking after him.*) Hallo ! What's the matter with him ? Cooling your heels, Peachey ? By George ! it's hot. Fancy the poor devils in London on a night like this, what ? [*He sees the moon.*] It's a full moon. You're lucky to be down here, Molly.

MRS. GWYN. [*In a low voice.*] Very !

MISS BEECH. Oh ! so you think she's lucky, do you ?

COLONEL. [*Expanding his nostrils.*] Delicious scent to night ! Hay and roses—delicious.

> [*He seats himself between them.*]

A shame that poor child has knocked up like this. Don't think it was the sun myself—more likely neuralgic—she's subject to neuralgia, Molly.

MRS. GWYN. [*Motionless.*] I know.

COLONEL. Got too excited about your coming. I told Nell not to keep worrying her about her frock, and this is the result. But your Aunt—you know—she can't let a thing alone !

MISS BEECH. Ah ! 'tisn't neuralgia.

> [MRS. GWYN *looks at her quickly and averts her eyes.*

COLONEL. Excitable little thing. You don't understand her, Peachey.

MISS BEECH. Don't I ?

COLONEL. She's all affection. Eh, Molly ? I re-

member what I was like at her age, a poor affectionate
little rat, and now look at me !

Miss Beech. [*Fanning herself.*] I see you.

Colonel. [*A little sadly.*] We forget what we were
like when we were young. She's been looking forward to to-night ever since you wrote; and now to
have to go to bed and miss the dancing. Too
bad !

Mrs. Gwyn. Don't, Uncle Tom !

Colonel. [*Patting her hand.*] There, there, old
girl, don't think about it. She'll be all right to-
morrow.

Miss Beech. If I were her mother I'd soon have
her up.

Colonel. Have her up with that headache ! What
are you talking about, Peachey ?

Miss Beech. *I* know a remedy.

Colonel. Well, out with it.

Miss Beech. Oh ! Molly knows it too !

Mrs. Gwyn. [*Staring at the ground.*] It's easy to
advise.

Colonel. [*Fidgeting.*] Well, if you're thinking of
morphia for her, don't have anything to do with it.
I've always set my face against morphia; the only
time I took it was in Burmah. I'd raging neuralgia
for two days. I went to our old doctor, and I made
him give me some. " Look here, doctor," I said,
" I hate the idea of morphia, I've never taken it,
and I never want to."

Miss Beech. [*Looking at Miss Gwyn.*] When a

tooth hurts, you should have it out.   It's only puttin'
off the evil day.

COLONEL. You say that because it wasn't your own.

MISS BEECH. Well, it was hollow, and you broke
your principles!

COLONEL. Hollow yourself, Peachey; you're as bad
as any one!

MISS BEECH [*With devilry.*] Well, I know that!
[*She turns to* MRS. GWYN.] He should have had it
out!   Shouldn't he, Molly?

MRS. GWYN. I—don't—judge for other people.

> [*She gets up suddenly, as though deprived of
> air.*

COLONEL. [*Alarmed.*] Hallo, Molly! Aren't *you*
feeling the thing, old girl?

MISS BEECH. Let her get some air, poor creature!

COLONEL. [*Who follows anxiously.*] Your Aunt's
got some first-rate sal volatile.

MRS. GWYN. It's all right, Uncle Tom.   I felt
giddy, it's nothing, now.

COLONEL. That's the dancing. [*He taps his forehead.*] I know what it is when you're not used to it.

MRS. GWYN. [*With a sudden bitter outburst.*] I suppose you think I'm a very bad mother to be amusing
myself while Joy's suffering.

COLONEL. My dear girl, whatever put such a
thought into your head? We all know if there were
anything you *could* do, you'd do it at once, wouldn't
she, Peachey?

> [MISS BEECH *turns a slow look on* MRS. GWYN.

Mrs. Gwyn. Ah! you see, Peachey knows me better.

Colonel. [*Following up his thoughts.*] I always think women are wonderful. There's your Aunt, she's very funny, but if there's anything the matter with me, she'll sit up all night; but when she's ill herself, and you try to do anything for her, out she raps at once.

Mrs. Gwyn [*In a low voice.*] There's always *one* that a woman will do anything for.

Colonel. Exactly what I say. With your Aunt it's me, and by George! Molly, sometimes I wish it wasn't.

Miss Beech. [*With meaning.*] But is it ever for another *woman* !

Colonel. You old cynic! D'you mean to say Joy wouldn't do anything on earth for her Mother, or Molly for Joy? You don't know human nature. What a wonderful night! Haven't seen such a moon for years, she's like a great, great lamp !

> [Mrs. Gwyn *hiding from* Miss Beech's *eyes,*
> *rises and slips her arm through his ; they*
> *stand together looking at the moon.*]

Don't like these Chinese lanterns, with that moon— tawdry! eh! By Jove, Molly, I sometimes think we humans are a rubbishy lot—each of us talking and thinking of nothing but our own potty little affairs ; and when you see a great thing like that up there —— [*Sighs.*] But there's your Aunt, if I were to say a thing like that to her she'd—she'd think me a lunatic; and yet, you know, she's a *very good* woman.

Mrs. Gwyn. [*Half clinging to him.*] Do *you* think me very selfish, Uncle Tom?

Colonel. My dear—what a fancy! Think you selfish—of *course* I don't; why should I?

Mrs. Gwyn. [*Dully.*] I don't know.

Colonel. [*Changing the subject nervously.*] I like your friend, Lever, Molly. He came to me before dinner quite distressed about your Aunt, beggin' me not to take those shares. She'll be the first to worry me, but he made such a point of it, poor chap—in the end I was obliged to say I wouldn't. I thought it showed very nice feeling. [*Ruefully.*] It's a pretty tight fit to make two ends meet on my income—I've missed a good thing, all owing to your Aunt. [*Dropping his voice.*] I don't mind telling you, Molly, I think they've got a much finer mine there than they've any idea of.

> [Mrs. Gwyn *gives way to laughter that is very near to sobs.*

[*With dignity.*] I can't see what there is to laugh at.

Mrs. Gwyn. I don't know what's the matter with me this evening.

Miss Beech. [*In a low voice.*] *I* do.

Colonel. There, there! Give me a kiss, old girl! [*He kisses her on the brow.*] Why, you're forehead's as hot as fire. I know—I know—you're fretting about Joy. Never mind—come! [*He draws her hand beneath*

his arm.] Let's go and have a look at the moon on
the river. We all get upset at times ; eh ! [*Lifting
his hand as if he had been stung.*] Why, you're not crying, Molly ! I say ! Don't do that, old girl, it makes
me wretched. Look here, Peachey. [*Holding out the
hand on which the tear has dropped.*] This is dreadful !

MRS. GWYN. [*With a violent effort.*] It's all right,
Uncle Tom !

> [MISS BEECH *wipes her own eyes stealthily.*
> *From the house is heard the voice of* MRS.
> HOPE, *calling* "TOM."

MISS BEECH. Some one calling you !

COLONEL. There, there, my dear, you just stay
here, and cool yourself—I'll come back—shan't be a
minute.   [*He turns to go.*]

> [MRS. HOPE'S *voice sounds nearer.*]

[*Turning back.*] And Molly, old girl, don't you mind
anything I said. I don't remember what it was—it
must have been *something*, I suppose.

> [*He hastily retreats.*

MRS. GWYN. [*In a fierce low voice.*] Why do you
torture me?

MISS BEECH. [*Sadly.*] I don't want to torture you.

MRS. GWYN. But you do. D'you think I haven't
seen this coming—all these weeks. I knew she
must find out some time ! But even a day counts——

MISS BEECH. I don't understand why you brought
him down here.

MRS. GWYN. [*After staring at her, bitterly.*] When
day after day and night after night you've thought

of nothing but how to keep them both, you might a little want to prove that it was possible, mightn't you? But *you don't* understand—how should you? You've never been a mother! [*And fiercely.*] You've never had a lov——

[MISS BEECH *raises her face—it is all puckered.*] [*Impulsively.*] Oh, I didn't mean that, Peachey!

MISS BEECH. All right, my dear.

MRS. GWYN. I'm so dragged in two   [*She sinks into a chair.*] I knew it must come.

MISS BEECH. Does she know everything, Molly?

MRS. GWYN. She guesses.

MISS BEECH. [*Mournfully.*] It's either him or her then, my dear; one or the other you'll have to give up.

MRS. GWYN. [*Motionless.*] Life's very hard on women?

MISS BEECH. Life's only just beginning for that child, Molly.

MRS. GWYN. You don't care if it ends for *me!*

MISS BEECH. Is it as bad as that?

MRS. GWYN. Yes.

MISS BEECH. [*Rocking her body.*] Poor things! Poor things!

MRS. GWYN. Are you still fond of me?

MISS BEECH. Yes, yes, my dear, of course I am.

MRS. GWYN. In spite of my—wickedness?

[*She laughs*

MISS BEECH. Who am I to tell what's wicked and what isn't? God knows you're both like daughters to me

MRS. GWYN. [*Abruptly.*] I can't.

MISS BEECH. Molly.

MRS. GWYN. You don't know what you're asking.

MISS BEECH. If I could save you suffering, my dear, I would. I hate suffering, if it's only a fly, I hate it.

MRS. GWYN. [*Turning away from her.*] Life isn't fair. Peachey, go in and leave me alone.

> [*She leans back motionless.*
>
> [MISS BEECH *gets off her seat, and stroking* MRS. GWYN's *arm in passing goes silently away. In the opening of the wall she meets* LEVER *who is looking for his partner. They make way for each other.*

LEVER. [*Going up to* MRS. GYWN—*gravely.*] The next is our dance, Molly.

MRS. GWYN. [*Unmoving.*] Let's sit it out here, then.

> [LEVER *sits down.*

LEVER. I've made it all right with your Uncle.

MRS. GWYN. [*Dully.*] Oh?

LEVER. I spoke to him about the shares before dinner.

MRS. GWYN. Yes, he told me, thank you.

LEVER. There's nothing to worry over, dear.

MRS. GWYN. [*Passionately.*] What does it matter about the wretched shares *now*? I'm stifling.

> [*She throws her scarf off.*

LEVER. I don't understand what you mean by " now."

MRS. GWYN. Don't you?

LEVER. We weren't—Joy can't *know*—why should she? I don't believe for a minute——

MRS. GWYN. Because you don't want to.

LEVER. Do you mean she does?

MRS. GWYN. Her heart knows.

> [LEVER *makes a movement of discomfiture; suddenly* MRS. GWYN *looks at him as though to read his soul.*]

I seem to bring you nothing but worry, Maurice. Are you tired of me?

LEVER. [*Meeting her eyes.*] No, I am not.

MRS. GWYN. Ah, but would you tell me if you were?

LEVER. [*Softly.*] Sufficient unto the day is the evil thereof.

> [MRS. GWYN *struggles to look at him, then covers her face with her hands.*

MRS. GWYN. If I were to give you up, you'd forget me in a month.

LEVER. Why do you say such things?

MRS. GWYN. If only I could believe I was necessary to you!

LEVER. [*Forcing the fervour of his voice.*] But you are!

MRS. GWYN. Am I? [*With the ghost of a smile.*] Midsummer day!

> [*She gives a laugh that breaks into a sob.*
> [*The music of a waltz sounds from the house.*

LEVER. For God's sake, don't, Molly—I don't believe in going to meet trouble.

Mrs. Gwyn. It's staring me in the face.

Lever. Let the future take care of itself !

> [Mrs. Gwyn *has turned away her face, cover-*
> *ing it with her hands.*]

Don't, Molly ! [*Trying to pull her hands away.*]
Don't !

Mrs. Gwyn. Oh ! what *shall* I do ?

> [*There is a silence ; the music of the waltz*
> *sounds louder from the house.*]

[*Starting up.*] Listen ! One can't sit it out and
dance it too. Which is it to be, Maurice, dancing—
or sitting out ? It must be one or the other,
mustn't it ?

Lever. Molly ! Molly !

Mrs. Gwyn. Ah, my dear ! [*Standing away from
him as though to show herself.*] How long shall I keep
you ? This is all that's left of me. It's time I joined
the wallflowers. [*Smiling faintly.*] It's time I played
the mother, isn't it ? [*In a whisper.*] It'll be all
sitting out then.

Lever. Don't ! Let's go and dance, it'll do you
good.

> [*He puts his hands on her arms, and in a gust*
> *of passion kisses her lips and throat.*

Mrs. Gwyn. I can't give you up—I can't. Love
me, oh ! love me !

> [*For a moment they stand so ; then, with sudden*
> *remembrance of where they are, they move*
> *apart.*

Lever. Are you all right now, darling ?

MRS. GWYN. [*Trying to smile.*] Yes, dear—quite.

LEVER. Then let's go, and dance.   [*They go.*

> [*For a few seconds the hollow tree stands alone; then from the house* ROSE *comes and enters it. She takes out a bottle of champagne, wipes it, and carries it away; but seeing* MRS. GWYN's *scarf lying across the chair, she fingers it, and stops, listening to the waltz. Suddenly draping it round her shoulders, she seizes the bottle of champagne, and waltzes with abandon to the music, as though avenging a long starvation of her instincts. Thus dancing, she is surprised by* DICK, *who has come to smoke a cigarette and think, at the spot where he was told to "have a go."* ROSE, *startled, stops and hugs the bottle.*

DICK. It's not claret, Rose, I shouldn't warm it.

> [ROSE, *taking off the scarf, replaces it on the chair; then with the half-warmed bottle, she retreats.* DICK, *in the swing, sits thinking of his fate. Suddenly from behind the hollow tree, he sees* JOY *darting forward in her day dress with her hair about her neck, and her skirt all torn. As he springs towards her she turns at bay.*

DICK. Joy!

JOY. I want Uncle Tom.

DICK. [*In consternation.*] But ought you to have got up—I thought you were ill in bed; oughtn't you to be lying down?

Joy. I haven't *been* in bed. Where's Uncle Tom ?

Dick. But where have you been—your dress is all torn ? Look   [*He touches the torn skirt.*

Joy. [*Tearing it away.*] In the fields. Where's uncle Tom ?

Dick. Aren't you really ill then ?

[Joy *shakes her head.* Dick, *showing her the irises.*] Look at these. They were the best I could get !

Joy. Don't ! I want Uncle Tom !

Dick. Won't you take them ?

Joy. I've got something else to do.

Dick. [*With sudden resolution.*] What do you want the Colonel for ?

Joy. I want him.

Dick. Alone ?

Joy. Yes.

Dick. Joy, what *is* the matter ?

Joy. I've got something to tell him.

Dick. What ? [*With sudden inspiration.*] Is it about Lever ?

Joy. [*In a low voice.*] The mine.

Dick. The mine ?

Joy. It's not—not a proper one.

Dick. How do you mean, Joy ?

Joy. I overheard. I don't care, I listened. I wouldn't if it had been anybody else, but I *hate* him.

Dick. [*Gravely.*] What did you hear ?

Joy. He's keeping back something Uncle Tom ought to know.

Dick. Are you sure?

> [Joy *makes a rush to pass him.*]
[*Barring the way.*]   No, wait a minute—you must!
Was it something that really matters, I don't
want to know what.

Joy. Yes, it was.

Dick. What a beastly thing—are you quite certain,
Joy?

Joy. [*Between her teeth.*]   Yes.

Dick. Then you *must* tell him, of course, even if
you did overhear.   You can't stand by and see the
Colonel swindled.   Whom was he talking to?

Joy. I won't tell you.

Dick. [*Taking her wrist.*] Was it—was it your
Mother?   [Joy *bends her head.*]
But if it was your Mother, why doesn't she——

Joy. Let me go!

Dick. [*Still holding her.*] I mean I can't see what—

Joy. [*Passionately.*] Let me *go!*

Dick. [*Releasing her.*] I'm thinking of your Mother
Joy.   She would never——

Joy. [*Covering her face.*] That man!

Dick. But Joy, just think!   There must be some
mistake.   It's so queer—it's *quite impossible!*

Joy. He won't let her.

Dick. Won't let her—won't *let* her?   But——
[*Stopping dead, and in a very different voice.*] Oh

Joy. [*Passionately.*] Why d'you look at me like
that?   Why can't you speak?

> [*She waits for him to speak, but he does not.*]

I'm going to show what he is, so that mother shan't speak to him again. I can—can't I—if I tell Uncle Tom?—can't I—— ?

DICK. But Joy—if your Mother knows a thing like —that——

JOY. She wanted to tell—she begged him—and he wouldn't.

DICK. But, Joy, dear, it means——

JOY. I hate him, I want to make her hate him, and I *will*.

DICK. But, Joy, dear, don't you see—if your Mother knows a thing like that, and doesn't speak of it, it means that she—it means that you can't *make* her hate him—it means—— If it were anybody else, but, well, you can't give *your own Mother* away !

JOY. How dare you! How *dare* you ! [*Turning to the hollow tree.*] It isn't true—— Oh ! it *isn't* true ?

DICK. [*In deep distress.*] Joy, dear, I never meant, I didn't really ! [*He tries to pull her hands down from her face.*

JOY. [*Suddenly.*] Oh! go away, go *away !*

> [MRS. GWYN *is seen coming back.* JOY *springs into the tree.* DICK *quickly steals away.* MRS. GWYN *goes up to the chair and takes the scarf that she has come for, and is going again when* JOY *steals out to her.*]

Mother ! [MRS. GWYN *stands looking at her with her teeth set on her lower lip.*]

Oh ! Mother, it isn't true ?

MRS. GWYN. [*Very still.*] What isn't true ?

Joy. That you and he are——

> [*Searching her Mother's face, which is deadly still. In a whisper*]

Then it *is* true.   Oh

Mrs. Gwyn. That's enough, Joy!   What *I* am *my* affair—not *yours*—do you understand ?

Joy. [*Low and fierce.*] Yes, I *do.*

Mrs. Gwyn. You don't.   You're only a child.

Joy. [*Passionately.*] I understand that you've hurt——   [*She stops.*

Mrs. Gwyn. Do you mean your father ?

Joy. [*Bowing her head.*] Yes, and—and me. [*She covers her face.*] I'm—I'm ashamed.

Mrs. Gwyn. I brought you into the world, and you say that to me ?   Have I been a bad mother to you ?

Joy. [*In a smothered voice.*] Oh ! Mother !

Mrs. Gwyn. Ashamed ?   Am *I* to live all my life like a dead woman because you're ashamed ?   Am I to live like the dead because you're a child that knows nothing of life ?   Listen, Joy, you'd better understand this once for all.   Your Father has no right over me and he knows it.   We've been hateful to each other for years.   *Can* you understand that ?   Don't cover your face like a child—look at me.

> [Joy *drops her hands, and lifts her face.* Mrs. Gwyn *looks back at her, her lips are quivering ; she goes on speaking with stammering rapidity.*]

D'you think—because I suffered when you were born and because I've suffered since with every ache you ever had, that that gives you the right to dictate to me now ? [*In a dead voice.*] I've been unhappy enough and I shall be unhappy enough in the time to come. [*Meeting the hard wonder in* Joy's *face.*] Oh ! you untouched things, you're as hard and cold as iron !

Joy. I would do anything for *you*, Mother.

Mrs. Gwyn. Except—let me live, Joy. That's the only thing you won't do for me, I quite understand.

Joy. Oh ! Mother, you *don't* understand—I *want* you so ; and I seem to be nothing to you now.

Mrs. Gwyn. Nothing to me ?   [*She smiles.*

Joy. Mother, darling, if you're so unhappy let's forget it all, let's go away and I'll be everything to you, I promise.

Mrs. Gwyn. [*With the ghost of a laugh.*] Ah, Joy !

Joy. I would try so hard.

Mrs. Gwyn. [*With the same quivering smile.*] My darling, I know you would, until you fell in love yourself.

Joy. Oh, Mother, I wouldn't, I never would, I swear it.

Mrs. Gwyn. There has never been a woman, Joy, that did not fall in love.

Joy. [*In a despairing whisper.*] But it's wrong of you—it's wicked !

Mrs. Gwyn. If it's wicked, *I* shall pay for it, not *you !*

Joy. But I want to save you, Mother !

Mrs. Gwyn. Save me ?   [*Breaking into laughter.*

Joy. I can't bear it that *you*—if you'll only—
I'll never leave you.   You think I don't know
what I'm saying, but I *do*, because even now I—
I half love somebody.   Oh, Mother! [*Pressing her
breast.*]   I feel—I feel *so awful*—as if everybody
knew.

Mrs. Gwyn. You think I'm a monster to hurt
you.   Ah! yes!   You'll understand better some
day.

Joy. [*In a sudden outburst of excited fear.*] I won't
believe   it—I—I—can't —you're *deserting   me*,
Mother.

Mrs. Gwyn. Oh, you untouched things! You——
        [Joy *looks up suddenly, sees her face, and sinks
            down on her knees.*

Joy. Mother—it's for *me!*

Mrs. Gwyn. Ask for my life, Joy—don't be
afraid!

        [Joy *turns her face away.*   Mrs. Gwyn *bends
            suddenly and touches her daughter's hair;*
            Joy *shrinks from that touch.*]

[*Recoiling as though she had been stung.*] I forgot—I'm
deserting you.

        [*And swiftly without looking back she goes away.*
            Joy *left alone under the hollow tree, crouches
            lower, and her shoulders shake.   Here* Dick
            *finds her, when he hears no longer any
            sound of voices.   He falls on his knees be-
            side her.*

Dick. Oh! Joy, dear, don't cry. It's so dreadful

        M

to see you! I'd do anything not to see you cry!
Say something.

> [Joy *is still for a moment, then the shaking of*
> *the shoulders begins again.*]

Joy, *darling!* It's so awful, you'll make yourself ill,
and it isn't worth it, really. I'd do anything to save
you pain—won't you stop just for a minute?

> [Joy *is still again.*]

Nothing in the world's worth *your* crying, Joy. Give
me just a little look

Joy. [*Looking; in a smothered voice*] Don't

Dick. You do look so sweet! Oh, Joy! I'll comfort you, I'll take it all on myself, I know all
about it.   [Joy *gives a sobbing laugh.*]
I do. I've had trouble too, I swear I have. It gets
better, it does really.

Joy. You don't know—it's—it's——

Dick. Don't think about it! No, no, no! I know
exactly what it's like.   [*He strokes her arm.*

Joy. [*Shrinking, in a whisper.*] You mustn't.

> [*The music of a waltz is heard again.*

Dick. Look here, Joy! It's no good, we must
talk it over calmly.

Joy. You don't *see!* It's the—it's the disgrace——

Dick. Oh! as to disgrace—she's *your* Mother,
whatever she does; I'd like to see anybody say anything about her—[*viciously*]—I'd punch his head.

Joy. [*Gulping her tears.*] That doesn't help.

Dick. But if she doesn't love your Father——

Joy. But she's *married* to him !

Dick. [*Hastily.*] Yes, of course, I know, marriage is awfully important ; but a man understands these things.

> [Joy *looks at him.   Seeing the impression he has made, he tries again.*]

I mean, he understands better than a woman.   I've often argued about moral questions with men up at Oxford.

Joy. [*Catching at a straw.*] But there's nothing to argue about.

Dick. [*Hastily.*] Of course, *I* believe in morals. [*They stare solemnly at each other.*] Some men don't. But *I* can't help seeing marriage is awfully important.

Joy. [*Solemnly.*] It's sacred.

Dick. Yes, I know, but there must be exceptions, Joy.

Joy. [*Losing herself a little in the stress of this discussion.*] How can there be exceptions if a thing's sacred ?

Dick. [*Earnestly.*] All rules have exceptions ; that's true, you know ; it's a proverb.

Joy. It can't be true about marriage—how can it when—— ?

Dick. [*With intense earnestness.*] But look here, Joy, I know a really clever man—an author.   He says that if marriage is a failure people ought to be perfectly free ; it isn't everybody who believes that marriage is everything.   Of course, *I* believe it's sacred, but if it's a failure, I *do* think it seems awful —don't you?

Joy. I don't know—yes—if—— [*Suddenly*] But *it's my own Mother!*

Dick. [*Gravely.*] I know, of course. I can't expect *you* to see it in *your own case* like this. [*With desperation.*] But look here, Joy, this'll show you! If a person loves a person, they have to decide, haven't they? Well, then, you see, that's what your Mother's done.

Joy. But that doesn't show me anything!

Dick. But it does. The thing is to look at it as if it wasn't yourself. If it had been you and me in love, Joy, and it was wrong, like them, of course [*ruefully*] I know you'd have decided right. [*Fiercely.*] But I swear I should have decided wrong. [*Triumphantly.*] That's why I feel I understand your Mother.

Joy. [*Brushing her sleeve across her eyes.*] Oh, Dick, you are so sweet—and—and—funny!

Dick. [*Sliding his arm about her.*] I love you, Joy, that's why, and I'll love you till you don't feel it any more. I will. I'll love you all day and every day; you shan't miss anything, I swear it. It's such a beautiful night—it's on purpose. Look! [Joy *looks; he looks at her.*] But it's not so beautiful as you.

Joy. [*Bending her head.*] You mustn't. I don't know—what's coming.

Dick. [*Sidling closer.*] Aren't your knees tired, darling? I—I *can't* get near you properly.

Joy. [*With a sob.*] Oh! Dick, you are a funny—comfort!

Dick. We'll stick together, Joy, always; nothing'll matter then.

> [*They struggle to their feet—the waltz sounds louder.*]

You're missing it all! I can't bear you to miss the dancing. It seems so queer! Couldn't we? Just a *little turn*?

Joy. No, no '

Dick. Oh ' try!

> [*He takes her gently by the waist, she shrinks back.*

Joy. [*Brokenly.*] No—no! Oh! Dick—to-morrow'll be so awful.

Dick. To-morrow shan't hurt you, Joy; nothing shall ever hurt *you* again.

> [*She looks at him, and her face changes ; suddenly she buries it against his shoulder.*
>
> [*They stand so just a moment in the moonlight ; then turning to the river move slowly out of sight. Again the hollow tree is left alone. The music of the waltz has stopped. The voices of* Miss Beech *and the* Colonel *are heard approaching from the house. They appear in the opening of the wall. The* Colonel *carries a pair of field-glasses with which to look at the moon.*

Colonel. Charming to see Molly dance with Lever,

their steps go so well together! I can always tell
when a woman's enjoying herself, Peachey.

Miss Beech. [*Sharply.*] Can you? You're *very*
clever.

Colonel. Wonderful, that moon! I'm going to
have a look at her! Splendid glasses these, Peachey
[*he screws them out*], not a better pair in England. I
remember in Burmah with these glasses I used to be
able to tell a man from a woman at two miles and a
quarter. And that's no joke, I can tell you. [*But
on his way to the moon, he has taken a survey of the earth
to the right along the river. In a low but excited voice*] I
say, I say—is it one of the maids?—the baggage!
Why! It's Dick! By George, she's got her hair
down, Peachey! It's *Joy!*

> [Miss Beech *goes to look. He makes as though
> to hand the glasses to her, but puts them to
> his own eyes instead—excitedly.*]

It is! What about her headache? By George,
they're kissing. I *say*, Peachey! I shall have to tell
Nell!

Miss Beech. Are you sure they're kissing? Well
that's some comfort.

Colonel. They're at the stile now. Oughtn't I
to stop them, eh? [*He stands on tiptoe.*] We mustn't
spy on them, dash it all. [*He drops the glasses.*]
They're out of sight now.

Miss Beech. [*To herself.*] He said he wouldn't let
her.

Colonel. *What!* have *you* been encouraging them!

Miss Beech. Don't be in such a hurry !

[*She moves towards the hollow tree.*

Colonel. [*Abstractedly.*] By George, Peachey, to think that Nell and I were once—Poor Nell ! I remember just such a night as this——

[*He stops, and stares before him, sighing.*

Miss Beech. [*Impressively.*] It's a comfort she's got that good young man. She's found out that her mother and this Mr. Lever are—*you* know.

Colonel. [*Losing all traces of his fussiness, and drawing himself up as though he were on parade.*] You tell me that my niece—— ?

Miss Beech. Out of her own mouth !

Colonel. [*Bowing his head.*] I never would have believed she'd have forgotten herself.

Miss Beech. [*Very solemnly.*] Ah, my dear ! We're all the same ; we're all as hollow as that tree ! When it's ourselves it's always a *special case !*

[*The* Colonel *makes a movement of distress, and* Miss Beech *goes to him.*]

Don't you take it so to heart, my dear !   [*A silence.*

Colonel. [*Shaking his head.*] I couldn't have be-lieved Molly would forget that child.

Miss Beech. [*Sadly.*] They must go their own ways, poor things ! She can't put herself in the child's place, and the child can't put herself in Molly's. A woman and a girl—there's the tree of life between them !

Colonel. [*Staring into the tree to see indeed if that were the tree alluded to.*] It's a grief to me, Peachey, it's a grief ! [*He sinks into a chair, stroking his long moustaches. Then to avenge his hurt.*] Shan't tell Nell—dashed if I do anything to make the trouble worse !

MISS BEECH. [*Nodding.*] There's suffering enough, without adding to it with our trumpery judgments ! If only things would last between them !

COLONEL. [*Fiercely.*] Last ! By George, they'd better—— [*He stops, and looking up with a queer sorry look.*] I say, Peachey—*Life's very funny !*

MISS BEECH. Men and women are ! [*Touching his forehead tenderly.*] There, there—take care of your poor, dear head ! Tsst ! The blessed innocents !

> [*She pulls the* COLONEL's *sleeve. They slip away towards the house, as* JOY *and* DICK *come back. They are still linked together, and stop by the hollow of the tree.*]

JOY. [*In a whisper.*] Dick, is love always like this !

DICK. [*Putting his arms round her, with conviction.*] *It's never been like this before. It's you and me !*

> [*He kisses her on the lips.*]

The curtain falls.

STRIFE

A DRAMA IN THREE ACTS

PERSONS OF THE PLAY

JOHN ANTHONY, *Chairman of the Trenartha Tin Plate Works*

EDGAR ANTHONY, *his son,*
FREDERIC H. WILDER,
WILLIAM SCANTLEBURY, } *Directors of the same*
OLIVER WANKLIN,

HENRY TENCH, *Secretary of the same*

FRANCIS UNDERWOOD, C.E., *Manager of the same*

SIMON HARNESS, *a Trade Union official*

DAVID ROBERTS,
JAMES GREEN,
JOHN BULGIN, } *the workmen's committee*
HENRY THOMAS
GEORGE ROUS,

HENRY ROUS,
LEWIS,
JAGO,
EVANS, } *workmen at the Trenartha Tin*
A BLACKSMITH, *Plate Works*
DAVIES,
A RED-HAIRED YOUTH,
BROWN,

FROST, *valet to John Anthony*

ENID UNDERWOOD, *wife of Francis Underwood, daughter John Anthony*

ANNIE ROBERTS, *wife of David Roberts*

MADGE THOMAS, *daughter of Henry Thomas*

MRS. ROUS, *mother of George and Henry Rous*

MRS. BULGIN, *wife of John Bulgin*

MRS. YEO, *wife of a workman*

A PARLOURMAID *to the Underwoods*

JAN, *Madge's brother, a boy of ten*

A CROWD OF MEN ON STRIKE

ACT I.,   *The dining-room of the Manager's house.*

ACT II.,   *SCENE I.*   *The kitchen of the Roberts' cottage*
                                    near the works.

                    SCENE II.   A space outside the works.

ACT III.,   The drawing-room of the Manager's house.

*The action takes place on February 7th between the hours of
noon and six in the afternoon, close to the Trenartha Tin Plate
Works, on the borders of England and Wales, where a strike
has been in progress throughout the winter.*

CAST OF THE ORIGINAL PRODUCTION

JOHN ANTHONY .	*Mr. Norman McKinnel*
EDGAR ANTHONY	*Mr. C. M. Halland*
FREDERIC WILDER	*Mr. Dennis Eadie*
WILLIAM SCANTLEBURY	*Mr. Luigi Lablache*
OLIVER WANKLIN	*Mr. Charles V. France*
HENRY TENCH .	*Mr. O. P. Heggie*
FRANCIS UNDERWOOD	*Mr. A. A. Holmwood*
SIMON HARNESS .	*Mr. George Ingleton*
DAVID ROBERTS .	*Mr. J. Fisher White*
JAMES GREEN .	*Mr. R. Luisk*
JOHN BULGIN .	*Mr. P. L. Julian*
HENRY THOMAS .	*Mr. H. R. Hignett*
GEORGE ROUS .	*Mr. Owen Roughwood*
JAGO .	*Mr. Charles Dancers*
EVANS .	*Mr. William Pilling*
FROST .	*Mr. Edward Gwenn*
ENID UNDERWOOD	*Miss Ellen O'Mally*
ANNIE ROBERTS .	*Miss Mary Barton*
MADGE THOMAS .	*Miss Lillah McCarthy*
MRS. ROUS .	*Miss Rose Cazalet*
MRS. BULGIN	*Miss Sidney Paxton*
MRS. YEO .	*Miss Blanche Stanley*

ACT I

*It is noon.   In the Underwoods' dining-room a bright fire
is burning.   On one side of the fireplace are double-
doors leading to the drawing-room, on the other side a
door leading to the hall.   In the centre of the room
a long dining-table without a cloth is set out as a board
table.   At the head of it, in the Chairman's seat, sits
JOHN ANTHONY, an old man, big, clean shaven, and
high-coloured, with thick white hair, and thick dark
eyebrows.   His movements are rather slow and feeble,
but his eyes are very much alive.   There is a glass
of water by his side.   On his right sits his son EDGAR,
an earnest-looking man of thirty, reading a newspaper.   Next him WANKLIN, a man with jutting eyebrows, and silver-streaked light hair, is bending over
transfer papers.   TENCH, the secretary, a short and
rather humble, nervous man, with side whiskers, stands
helping him.   On WANKLIN's right sits UNDERWOOD,
the Manager, a quiet man, with a long, stiff jaw, and
steady eyes.   Back to the fire is SCANTLEBURY, a very
large, pale, sleepy man, with grey hair, rather bald.
Between him and the Chairman are two empty chairs.*

WILDER. [*Who is lean, cadaverous, and complaining,
with drooping grey moustaches, stands before the fire.*]

189

I say, this fire's the devil! Can I have a screen, Tench?

SCANTLEBURY. A screen, ah!

TENCH. Certainly, Mr. Wilder. [*He looks at* UNDER-WOOD.] That is—perhaps the Manager—perhaps Mr. Underwood——

SCANTLEBURY. These fireplaces of yours, Underwood——

UNDERWOOD [*Roused from studying some papers.*] A screen? Rather! I'm sorry. [*He goes to the door with a little smile.*] We're not accustomed to complaints of too much fire down here just now.

> [*He speaks as though he holds a pipe between his teeth, slowly, ironically.*

WILDER. [*In an injured voice.*] You mean the men. H'm! [UNDERWOOD *goes out.*

SCANTLEBURY. Poor devils!

WILDER. It's their own fault, Scantlebury.

EDGAR. [*Holding out his paper.*] There's great distress amongst them, according to the *Trenartha News.*

WILDER. Oh, that rag! Give it to Wanklin. Suit his Radical views. They call us monsters, I suppose. The editor of that rubbish ought to be shot.

EDGAR. [*Reading.*] " If the Board of worthy gentlemen who control the Trenartha Tin Plate Works from their armchairs in London, would condescend to come and see for themselves the conditions prevailing amongst their workpeople during this strike——"

WILDER. Well, we *have* come.

EDGAR. [*Continuing.*] "We cannot believe that
even their leg-of-mutton hearts would remain untouched." [WANKLIN *takes the paper from him.*

WILDER. Ruffian! I remember that fellow when
he hadn't a penny to his name; little snivel of a chap
that's made his way by blackguarding everybody who
takes a different view to himself.

[ANTHONY *says something that is not heard*
WILDER. What does your father say?

EDGAR. He says "The kettle and the pot."

WILDER. H'm! [*He sits down next to* SCANTLEBURY.

SCANTLEBURY. [*Blowing out his cheeks.*] I shall boil
if I don't get that screen.

[UNDERWOOD *and* ENID *enter with a screen,
which they place before the fire.* ENID *is tall;
she has a small, decided face, and is twenty-
eight years old.*

ENID. Put it closer, Frank. Will that do, Mr.
Wilder? It's the highest we've got.

WILDER. Thanks, capitally.

SCANTLEBURY. [*Turning, with a sigh of pleasure.*] Ah!
Merci, Madame'

ENID. Is there anything else you want, father?
[ANTHONY *shakes his head.*] Edgar—anything?

EDGAR. You might give me a "J" nib, old girl.

ENID. There are some down there by Mr. Scantlebury.

SCANTLEBURY. [*Handing a little box of nibs.*] Ah
your brother uses "J's." What does the manager
use? [*With expansive politeness.*] What does your
husband use, Mrs. Underwood?

UNDERWOOD. A quill!

SCANTLEBURY. The homely product of the goose.

[*He holds out quills.*

UNDERWOOD. [*Drily.*] Thanks, if you can spare me one. [*He takes a quill.*] What about lunch, Enid?

ENID. [*Stopping at the double doors and looking back.*] We're going to have lunch here, in the drawing-room, so you needn't hurry with your meeting.

[WANKLIN *and* WILDER *bow, and she goes out.*

SCANTLEBURY. [*Rousing himself, suddenly.*] Ah! Lunch! That hotel—— Dreadful! Did you try the whitebait last night? Fried fat!

WILDER. Past twelve! Aren't you going to read the minutes, Tench?

TENCH. [*Looking for the* CHAIRMAN'S *assent, reads in a rapid and monotonous voice*]. " At a Board Meeting held the 31st of January at the Company's Offices, 512, Cannon Street, E.C. Present—Mr. Anthony in the chair, Messrs. F. H. Wilder, William Scantlebury, Oliver Wanklin, and Edgar Anthony. Read letters from the Manager dated January 20th, 23rd, 25th, 28th, relative to the strike at the Company's Works. Read letters to the Manager of January 21st, 24th, 26th, 29th. Read letter from Mr. Simon Harness, of the Central Union, asking for an interview with the Board. Read letter from the Men's Committee, signed David Roberts, James Green, John Bulgin, Henry Thomas, George Rous, desiring conference with the Board; and it was resolved that a special Board Meeting be called for February 7th at the house of the Manager, for the purpose of discussing the situation with Mr. Simon Harness and the Men's Committee on the spot.   Passed twelve transfers, signed and sealed nine certificates and one balance certificate."

[*He pushes the book over to the* CHAIRMAN.

ANTHONY. [*With a heavy sigh.*] If it's your pleasure, sign the same.

[*He signs, moving the pen with difficulty.*

WANKLIN. What's the Union's game, Tench? They haven't made up their split with the men. What does Harness want this interview for?

TENCH. Hoping we shall come to a compromise, I think, sir; he's having a meeting with the men this afternoon.

WILDER. Harness!   Ah!   He's one of those cold-blooded, cool-headed chaps.   I distrust them.   I don't know that we didn't make a mistake to come down.   What time'll the men be here?

UNDERWOOD. Any time now.

WILDER. Well, if we're not ready, they'll have to wait—won't do 'em any harm to cool their heels a bit.

SCANTLEBURY. [*Slowly.*] Poor devils!   It's snowing. *What* weather!

UNDERWOOD. [*With meaning slowness.*] This house'll be the warmest place they've been in this winter.

WILDER. Well, I hope we're going to settle this business in time for me to catch the 6.30.   I've got to take my wife to Spain to-morrow. [*Chattily.*] My

N

old father had a strike at his works in '69 ; just such a February as this.   They wanted to shoot him.

WANKLIN. What ! In the close season ?

WILDER. By George, there was no close season for employers then !   He used to go down to his office with a pistol in his pocket.

SCANTLEBURY. [*Faintly alarmed.*] Not seriously ?

WILDER. [*With finality.*] Ended in his shootin' one of 'em in the legs.

SCANTLEBURY. [*Unavoidably feeling his thigh.*] No ? Which ?

ANTHONY. [*Lifting the agenda paper.*] To consider the policy of the Board in relation to the strike.

[*There is a silence.*

WILDER. It's this infernal three-cornered duel— the Union, the men, and ourselves.

WANKLIN. We needn't consider the Union.

WILDER. It's my experience that you've always got to consider the Union, confound them !   If the Union were going to withdraw their support from the men, as they've done, why did they ever allow them to strike at all ?

EDGAR. We've had that over a dozen times.

WILDER. Well, I've never understood it !   It's beyond me.   They talk of the engineers' and fur-nacemen's demands being excessive—so they are— but that's not enough to make the Union withdraw their support.   What's behind it ?

UNDERWOOD. Fear of strikes at Harper's and Tinewell's.

WILDER. [*With triumph.*] Afraid of other strikes—
now, that's a reason! Why couldn't we have been
told that before?

UNDERWOOD. You were.

TENCH. You were absent from the Board that day,
sir.

SCANTLEBURY. The men must have seen they had
no chance when the Union gave them up. It's
madness.

UNDERWOOD. It's Roberts!

WILDER. Just our luck, the men finding a fanatical
firebrand like Roberts for leader.   [*A pause.*

WANKLIN. [*Looking at* ANTHONY.] Well?

WILDER. [*Breaking in fussily.*] It's a regular mess.
I don't like the position we're in; I don't like it;
I've said so for a long time. [*Looking at* WANKLIN.]
When Wanklin and I came down here before Christ-
mas it looked as if the men must collapse. You
thought so too, Underwood.

UNDERWOOD. Yes.

WILDER. Well, they haven't! Here we are, going
from bad to worse—losing our customers—shares
going down!

SCANTLEBURY. [*Shaking his head.*] M'm! M'm!

WANKLIN. What loss have we made by this strike,
Tench?

TENCH. Over fifty thousand, sir!

SCANTLEBURY. [*Pained.*] You don't say!

WILDER. We shall never get it back.

TENCH. No, sir.

WILDER. Who'd have supposed the men were going to stick out like this—nobody suggested that. [*Looking angrily at* TENCH.]

SCANTLEBURY. [*Shaking his head.*] I've never liked a fight—never shall.

ANTHONY. No surrender !   [*All look at him.*

WILDER. Who wants to surrender ? [ANTHONY *looks at him.*] I—I want to act reasonably. When the men sent Roberts up to the Board in December—then was the time. We ought to have humoured him ; instead of that, the Chairman—[*Dropping his eyes before* ANTHONY's]—er—we snapped his head off. We could have got them in then by a little tact.

ANTHONY. No compromise !

WILDER. There we are ! This strike's been going on now since October, and as far as I can see it may last another six months. Pretty mess we shall be in by then. The only comfort is, the men'll be in a worse !

EDGAR. [*To* UNDERWOOD.] What sort of state are they really in, Frank ?

UNDERWOOD. [*Without expression.*] Damnable !

WILDER. Well, who on earth would have thought they'd have held on like this without support !

UNDERWOOD. Those who know them.

WILDER. I defy any one to know them ! And what about tin? Price going up daily. When we do get started we shall have to work off our contracts at the top of the market.

WANKLIN. What do you say to that, Chairman ?

ANTHONY. Can't be helped!

WILDER. Shan't pay a dividend till goodness knows when!

SCANTLEBURY. [*With emphasis.*] We ought to think of the shareholders. [*Turning heavily.*] Chairman, I say we ought to think of the shareholders.

[ANTHONY *mutters.*

SCANTLEBURY. What's that?

TENCH. The Chairman says he *is* thinking of you, sir.

SCANTLEBURY. [*Sinking back into torpor.*] Cynic!

WILDER. It's past a joke. *I* don't want to go without a dividend for years if the Chairman does. We can't go on playing ducks and drakes with the Company's prosperity.

EDGAR. [*Rather ashamedly.*] I think we ought to consider the men.

[*All but* ANTHONY *fidget in their seats.*

SCANTLEBURY. [*With a sigh.*] We mustn't think of our private feelings, young man. That'll never do.

EDGAR. [*Ironically.*] I'm not thinking of our feelings. I'm thinking of the men's.

WILDER. As to that—we're men of business.

WANKLIN. That *is* the little trouble.

EDGAR. There's no necessity for pushing things so far in the face of all this suffering—it's—it's cruel.

[*No one speaks, as though* EDGAR *had uncovered
something whose existence no man prizing his
self-respect could afford to recognise.*

WANKLIN. [*With an ironical smile.*] I'm afraid we mustn't base our policy on luxuries like sentiment.

EDGAR. I detest this state of things.

ANTHONY. We didn't seek the quarrel.

EDGAR. I know that, sir, but surely we've gone far enough.

ANTHONY. No.   [*All look at one another.*

WANKLIN. Luxuries apart, Chairman, we must look out what we're doing.

ANTHONY. Give way to the men once and there'll be no end to it.

WANKLIN. I quite agree, but——

[ANTHONY *shakes his head.*]

You make it a question of bedrock principle?

[ANTHONY *nods.*]

Luxuries again, Chairman ! The shares are below par.

WILDER. Yes, and they'll drop to a half when we pass the next dividend.

SCANTLEBURY. [*With alarm.*] Come, come ! Not so bad as that.

WILDER. [*Grimly.*] You'll see ! [*Craning forward to catch* ANTHONY's *speech.*] I didn't catch——

TENCH. [*Hesitating*] The Chairman says, sir, " Fais que—que—devra——"

EDGAR. [*Sharply.*] My father says : " Do what we ought—and let things rip."

WILDER. Tcha !

SCANTLEBURY. [*Throwing up his hands.*] The Chairman's a Stoic—I always said the Chairman was a Stoic.

WILDER. Much good that'll do us.

WANKLIN. [*Suavely.*] Seriously, Chairman, are you going to let the ship sink under you, for the sake of—a principle ?

ANTHONY. She won't sink.

SCANTLEBURY. [*With alarm.*] Not while I'm on the Board I hope.

ANTHONY. [*With a twinkle.*] Better rat, Scantlebury.

SCANTLEBURY. What a man !

ANTHONY. I've always fought them ; I've never been beaten yet.

WANKLIN. We're with you in theory, Chairman. But we're not all made of cast-iron.

ANTHONY.   We've only to hold on.

WILDER. [*Rising and going to the fire.*] And go to the devil as fast as we can !

ANTHONY. Better go to the devil than give in !

WILDER. [*Fretfully.*] That may suit you, sir, but it doesn't suit me, or any one else I should think.

[ANTHONY *looks him in the face—a silence.*

EDGAR. I don't see how we can get over it that to go on like this means starvation to the men's wives and families.

[WILDER *turns abruptly to the fire, and* SCANTLEBURY *puts out a hand to push the idea away.*

WANKLIN. I'm afraid again that sounds a little sentimental.

EDGAR. Men of business are excused from decency, you think ?

WILDER. Nobody's more sorry for the men than I am, but if they [*lashing himself*] choose to be such a pig-headed lot, it's nothing to do with us; we've quite enough on *our* hands to think of ourselves and the shareholders.

EDGAR. [*Irritably.*] It won't kill the shareholders to miss a dividend or two; I don't see that *that's* reason enough for knuckling under.

SCANTLEBURY. [*With grave discomfort.*] You talk very lightly of your dividends, young man; I don't know where we are.

WILDER. There's only one sound way of looking at it. We can't go on ruining *ourselves* with this strike.

ANTHONY. No caving in !

SCANTLEBURY. [*With a gesture of despair.*] Look at him !

> [ANTHONY *is leaning back in his chair. They do look at him.*

WILDER. [*Returning to his seat.*] Well, all I can say is, if that's the Chairman's view, I don't know what we've come down here for.

ANTHONY. To tell the men that we've got nothing for them—— [*Grimly.*] They won't believe it till they hear it spoken in plain English.

WILDER. H'm ! Shouldn't be a bit surprised if that brute Roberts hadn't got us down here with the very same idea. I hate a man with a grievance.

EDGAR. [*Resentfully.*] We didn't pay him enough for his discovery. I always said that at the time.

WILDER. We paid him five hundred and a bonus

of two hundred three years later. If that's not enough! What does he want for goodness' sake?

TENCH. [*Complainingly.*] Company made a hundred thousand out of his brains, and paid him seven hundred—that's the way he goes on, sir.

WILDER. The man's a rank agitator! Look here, I hate the Unions. But now we've got Harness here let's get him to settle the whole thing.

ANTHONY. No! [*Again they look at him.*]

UNDERWOOD. Roberts won't let the men assent to that.

SCANTLEBURY. Fanatic! Fanatic!

WILDER. [*Looking at* ANTHONY.] And not the only one! [FROST *enters from the hall.*]

FROST. [*To* ANTHONY.] Mr. Harness from the Union, waiting, sir. The men are here too, sir.

> [ANTHONY *nods.* UNDERWOOD *goes to the door, returning with* HARNESS, *a pale, clean-shaven man with hollow cheeks, quick eyes and lantern jaw*—FROST *has retired.*

UNDERWOOD. [*Pointing to* TENCH'S *chair.*] Sit there next the Chairman, Harness, won't you?

> [*At* HARNESS'S *appearance, the Board have drawn together, as it were, and turned a little to him, like cattle at a dog.*

HARNESS. [*With a sharp look round, and a bow.*] Thanks! [*He sits—his accent is slightly nasal.*] Well, Gentlemen, we're going to do business at last, I hope.

WILDER. Depends on what you *call* business, Harness. Why don't you make the men come in?

HARNESS. [*Sardonically.*] The men are far more in the right than you are. The question with us is whether we shan't begin to support them again.

> [*He ignores them all, except* ANTHONY, *to whom he turns in speaking.*

ANTHONY. Support them if you like ; we'll put in free labour and have done with it.

HARNESS. That won't do, Mr. Anthony. You can't get free labour, and you know it.

ANTHONY. We shall see that.

HARNESS. I'm quite frank with you. We were forced to withhold our support from your men because some of their demands are in excess of current rates. I expect to make them withdraw those demands to-day : if they do, take it straight from me, gentlemen, we shall back them again at once. Now, I want to see something fixed up before I go back to-night. Can't we have done with this old-fashioned tug-of-war business ? What good's it doing you ? Why don't you recognise once for all that these people are men like yourselves, and want what's good for them just as you want what's good for you—— [*Bitterly.*] Your motor-cars, and champagne, and eight-course dinners.

ANTHONY. If the men will come in, we'll do some-them for them.

HARNESS. [*Ironically.*] Is that your opinion too, sir—and yours—and yours? [*The Directors do not answer.*] Well, all I can say is: It's a kind of high and mighty aristocratic tone I thought we'd grown out of—seems I was mistaken.

ANTHONY. It's the tone the men use. Remains to be seen which can hold out longest—they without us, or we without them.

HARNESS. As business men, I wonder you're not ashamed of this waste of force, gentlemen. You know what it'll all end in.

ANTHONY. What ?

HARNESS. Compromise—it always does.

SCANTLEBURY. Can't you persuade the men that their interests are the same as ours ?

HARNESS. [*Turning, ironically.*] I could persuade them of that, sir, if they were.

WILDER. Come Harness, you're a clever man, you don't believe all the Socialistic claptrap that's talked nowadays. There's no real difference between their interests and ours.

HARNESS. There's just one very simple little question I'd like to put to you. Will you pay your men one penny more than they force you to pay them ?

[WILDER *is silent.*

WANKLIN. [*Chiming in.*] I humbly thought that not to pay more than was necessary was the A B C of commerce.

HARNESS. [*With irony.*] Yes, that seems to be the A B C of commerce, sir ; and the A B C of commerce is between your interests and the men's.

SCANTLEBURY. [*Whispering.*] We ought to arrange something.

HARNESS. [*Drily.*] Am I to understand then, gentlemen, that your Board is going to make no concessions ?

> [WANKLIN *and* WILDER *bend forward as if to speak, but stop.*

ANTHONY. [*Nodding.*] None.

> [WANKLIN *and* WILDER *again bend forward, and* SCANTLEBURY *gives an unexpected grunt.*

HARNESS. You were about to say something, I believe ?   [*But* SCANTLEBURY *says nothing.*

EDGAR. [*Looking up suddenly.*] We're sorry for the state of the men.

HARNESS. [*Icily.*] The men have no use for your pity, sir.   What they want is justice.

ANTHONY. Then let *them* be just.

HARNESS. For that word "just" read "humble," Mr. Anthony.   Why should they be humble?   Barring the accident of money, aren't they as good men as you ?

ANTHONY. Cant!

HARNESS. Well, I've been five years in America. It colours a man's notions.

SCANTLEBURY. [*Suddenly, as though avenging his uncompleted grunt.*] Let's have the men in and hear what they've got to say !

> [ANTHONY *nods, and* UNDERWOOD *goes out by the single door.*

HARNESS. [*Drily.*] As I'm to have an interview with them this afternoon, gentlemen, I'll ask you to postpone your final decision till that's over.

[*Again* ANTHONY *nods, and taking up his glass drinks.*

[UNDERWOOD *comes in again, followed by* ROBERTS, GREEN, BULGIN, THOMAS, ROUS. *They file in, hat in hand, and stand silent in a row.* ROBERTS *is lean, of middle height, with a slight stoop. He has a little rat-gnawn, brown-grey beard, moustaches, high cheek bones, hollow cheeks, small fiery eyes. He wears an old and grease-stained, blue serge suit, and carries an old bowler hat. He stands nearest the Chairman.* GREEN, *next to him, has a clean, worn face, with a small grey, goatee beard and drooping moustaches, iron spectacles, and mild, straight-forward eyes. He wears an overcoat, green with age, and a linen collar. Next to him is* BULGIN, *a tall, strong man, with a dark moustache, and fighting jaw, wearing a red muffler, who keeps changing his cap from one hand to the other. Next to him is* THOMAS, *an old man with a grey moustache, full beard, and weatherbeaten, bony face, whose overcoat discloses a lean, plucked-looking neck. On his right,* ROUS, *the youngest of the five, looks like a soldier; he has a glitter in his eyes.*

UNDERWOOD. [*Pointing.*] There are some chairs there against the wall, Roberts; won't you draw them up and sit down?

ROBERTS. Thank you, Mr. Underwood we'll stand—in the presence of the Board. [*He speaks in a biting and staccato voice, rolling his r's, pronouncing his a's like an Italian a, and his consonants short and crisp.*] How are you, Mr. Harness? Didn't expect t' have the pleasure of seeing you till this afternoon.

HARNESS. [*Steadily.*] We shall meet again then, Roberts.

ROBERTS. Glad to hear that; we shall have some news for you to take to your people.

ANTHONY. What do the men want?

ROBERTS. [*Acidly.*] Beg pardon, I don't quite catch the Chairman's remark.

TENCH. [*From behind the Chairman's chair.*] The Chairman wishes to know what the men have to say.

ROBERTS. It's what the Board has to say we've come to hear. It's for the Board to speak first.

ANTHONY. The Board has nothing to say.

ROBERTS. [*Looking along the line of men.*] In that case we're wasting the Directors' time. We'll be taking our feet off this pretty carpet.

[*He turns, the men move slowly, as though hypnotically influenced.*

WANKLIN. [*Suavely.*] Come Roberts, you didn't give us this long cold journey for the pleasure of saying that.

THOMAS. [*A pure Welshman.*] No, sir, an' what I say iss——

ROBERTS. [*Bitingly.*] Go on, Henry Thomas, go

on. You're better able to speak to the—Directors than me.   [Thomas *is silent.*

TENCH. The Chairman means, Roberts, that it was the men who asked for the Conference, the Board wish to hear what they have to say.

ROBERTS. Gad ! If I was to begin to tell ye all they have to say, I wouldn't be finished to-day. And there'd be some that'd wish they'd never left their London palaces.

HARNESS. What's your proposition, man ?   Be reasonable.

ROBERTS. You want reason, Mr. Harness ?   Take a look round this afternoon before the meeting. [*He looks at the men ; no sound escapes them.*]   You'll see some very pretty scenery.

HARNESS. All right, my friend ; you won't put me off.

ROBERTS. [*To the men.*]   We shan't put Mr. Harness off.   Have some champagne with your lunch, Mr. Harness ; you'll want it, sir.

HARNESS. Come, get to business, man !

THOMAS. What we're asking, look you, is just simple justice.

ROBERTS. [*Venomously.*]   Justice from London ? What are you talking about, Henry Thomas ?   Have you gone silly ? [Thomas *is silent.*]   We know very well what we are—discontented dogs—never satisfied. What did the Chairman tell me up in London ?   That I didn't know what I was talking about.   I was a foolish, uneducated man, that knew nothing of the wants of the men I spoke for.

EDGAR. Do please keep to the point.

ANTHONY. [*Holding up his hand.*] There can only be one master, Roberts.

ROBERTS. Then, be Gad, it'll be us.

[*There is a silence;* ANTHONY *and* ROBERTS *stare at one another.*]

UNDERWOOD. If you've nothing to say to the Directors, Roberts, perhaps you'll let Green or Thomas speak for the men.

[GREEN *and* THOMAS *look anxiously at* ROBERTS, *at each other, and the other men.*]

GREEN. [*An Englishman.*] If I'd been listened to, gentlemen——

THOMAS. What I'fe got to say iss what we'fe all got to say——

ROBERTS. Speak for yourself, Henry Thomas.

SCANTLEBURY. [*With a gesture of deep spiritual discomfort.*] Let the poor men call their souls their own!

ROBERTS. Aye, they shall keep their souls, for it's not much body that you've left them, Mr. [*with biting emphasis, as though the word were an offence*] Scantlebury! [*To the men.*] Well, will you speak, or shall I speak for you?

ROUS. [*Suddenly.*] Speak out, Roberts, or leave it to others.

ROBERTS. [*Ironically.*] Thank you, George Rous. [*Addressing himself to* ANTHONY.] The Chairman and Board of Directors have honoured us by leaving London and coming all this way to hear what we've got to say; it would not be polite to keep them any longer waiting.

WILDER. Well, thank God for that!

ROBERTS. Ye will not dare to thank Him when I have done, Mr. Wilder, for all your piety. May be your God up in London has no time to listen to the working man. I'm told He is a wealthy God; but if He listens to what I tell Him, He will know more than ever He learned in Kensington.

HARNESS. Come, Roberts, you have your own God. Respect the God of other men.

ROBERTS. That's right, sir. We have another God down here; I doubt He is rather different to Mr. Wilder's. Ask Henry Thomas; he will tell you whether his God and Mr. Wilder's are the same.

> [THOMAS *lifts his hand, and cranes his head as though to prophecy.*

WANKLIN. For goodness' sake, let's keep to the point, Roberts.

ROBERTS. I rather think it is the point, Mr. Wanklin. If you can get the God of Capital to walk through the streets of Labour, and pay attention to what he sees, you're a brighter man than I take you for, for all that you're a Radical.

ANTHONY. Attend to me, Roberts! [ROBERTS *is silent.*] You are here to speak for the men, as I am here to speak for the Board.

> [*He looks slowly round.*

o

[WILDER, WANKLIN, *and* SCANTLEBURY *make
    movements of uneasiness, and* EDGAR *gazes
    at the floor. A faint smile comes on* HAR-
    NESS' *face*.]

Now then, what is it ?

ROBERTS. Right, sir !

[*Throughout all that follows, he and* ANTHONY
    *look fixedly upon each other. Men and
    Directors show in their various ways sup-
    pressed uneasiness, as though listening to words
    that they themselves would not have spoken.*]

The men can't afford to travel up to London;
and they don't trust you to believe what they
say in black and white. They know what the
post is [*he darts a look at* UNDERWOOD *and* TENCH],
and what Directors' meetings are : " Refer it to the
manager—let the manager advise us on the men's
condition. Can we squeeze them a little more ? "

UNDERWOOD. [*In a low voice*.] Don't hit below the
belt, Roberts !

ROBERTS. Is it below the belt, Mr. Underwood?
The men know. When I came up to London, I told
you the position straight. An' what came of it ? I
was told I didn't know what I was talkin' about. I
can't afford to travel up to London to be told that again.

ANTHONY. What have you to say for the men ?

ROBERTS. I have this to say—and first as to their
condition. Ye shall 'ave no need to go and ask your
manager. Ye can't squeeze them any more. Every
man of us is well-nigh starving. [*A surprised murmur*

rises from the men. ROBERTS *looks round.*] Ye wonder
why I tell ye that? Every man of us is going short.
We can't be no worse off than we've been these
weeks past. Ye needn't think that by waiting ye'll
drive us to come in. We'll die first, the whole lot of
us. The men have sent for ye to know, once and for
all, whether ye are going to grant them their demands. I see the sheet of paper in the Secretary's
hand. [TENCH *moves nervously.*] That's it, I think, Mr.
Tench. It's not very large.

TENCH. [*Nodding.*] Yes.

ROBERTS. There's not one sentence of writing on
that paper that we can do without.

> [*A movement amongst the men.* ROBERTS *turns
> on them sharply.*]

Isn't that so?

> [*The men assent reluctantly.* ANTHONY *takes
> from* TENCH *the paper and peruses it.*]

Not one single sentence. All those demands are
fair. We have not asked anything that we are not
entitled to ask. What I said up in London, I say
again now: there is not anything on that piece of
paper that a just man should not ask, and a just man
give.   [*A pause.*

ANTHONY. There is not one single demand on this
paper that we will grant.

> [*In the stir that follows on these words,* ROBERTS
> *watches the Directors and* ANTHONY *the men.*
> WILDER *gets up abruptly and goes over to
> the fire.*

ROBERTS. D'ye mean that?

ANTHONY. I do.

> [WILDER *at the fire makes an emphatic move-*
> *ment of disgust.*

ROBERTS. [*Noting it, with dry intensity.*] Ye best
know whether the condition of the Company is any
better than the condition of the men. [*Scanning the
Directors' faces.*] Ye best know whether ye can afford
your tyranny—but this I tell ye: If ye think the
men will give way the least part of an inch, ye're
making the worst mistake ye ever made. [*He fixes his
eyes on* SCANTLEBURY.] Ye think because the Union
is not supporting us—more shame to it !—that we'll
be coming on our knees to you one fine morning.
Ye think because the men have got their wives an'
families to think of—that it's just a question of a
week or two——

ANTHONY. It would be better if you did not specu-
late so much on what we think.

ROBERTS. Aye! It's not much profit to us! I will
say this for you, Mr. Anthony — ye know your
own mind! [*Staring at* ANTHONY.] I can reckon on
ye!

ANTHONY. [*Ironically.*] I am obliged to you!

ROBERTS. And I know mine. I tell ye this. The
men will send their wives and families where the
country will have to keep them; an' they will starve
sooner than give way. I advise ye, Mr. Anthony, to
prepare yourself for the worst that can happen to
your Company. We are not so ignorant as you might

suppose. We know the way the cat is jumping. Your position is not all that it might be—not exactly!

ANTHONY. Be good enough to allow us to judge of our position for ourselves. Go back, and re-consider your own.

ROBERTS. [*Stepping forward.*] Mr. Anthony, you are not a young man now; from the time that I remember anything ye have been an enemy to every man that has come into your works. I don't say that ye're a mean man, or a cruel man, but ye've grudged them the say of any word in their own fate. Ye've fought them down four times. I've heard ye say ye love a fight—mark my words—ye're fighting the last fight ye'll ever fight——

[TENCH *touches* ROBERTS' *sleeve.*

UNDERWOOD. Roberts! Roberts!

ROBERTS. Roberts! Roberts! I mustn't speak my mind to the Chairman, but the Chairman may speak his mind to me!

WILDER. What are things coming to?

ANTHONY. [*With a grim smile at* WILDER.] Go on, Roberts; say what you like!

ROBERTS. [*After a pause.*] I have no more to say.

ANTHONY. The meeting stands adjourned to five o'clock.

WANKLIN. [*In a low voice to* UNDERWOOD.] We shall never settle anything like this.

ROBERTS. [*Bitingly.*] We thank the Chairman

and Board of Directors for their gracious hearing.

> [*He moves towards the door; the men cluster together stupefied; then* ROUS, *throwing up his head, passes* ROBERTS *and goes out. The others follow.*

ROBERTS. [*With his hand on the door—maliciously.*] Good day, gentlemen!   [*He goes out.*

HARNESS. [*Ironically.*] I congratulate you on the conciliatory spirit that's been displayed. With your permission, gentlemen, I'll be with you again at half-past five. Good morning!

> [*He bows slightly, rests his eyes on* ANTHONY, *who returns his stare unmoved, and, followed by* UNDERWOOD, *goes out. There is a moment of uneasy silence.* UNDERWOOD *re-appears in the doorway.*

WILDER. [*With emphatic disgust*]. Well!

> [*The double doors are opened.*

ENID. [*Standing in the doorway.*] Lunch is ready.

> [EDGAR, *getting up abruptly, walks out past his sister.*

WILDER. Coming to lunch, Scantlebury?

SCANTLEBURY. [*Rising heavily.*] I suppose so, I suppose so. It's the only thing we can do.

> [*They go out through the double doors.*

WANKLIN. [*In a low voice.*] Do you really mean to fight to a finish, Chairman?   [ANTHONY *nods.*

WANKLIN. Take care! The essence of things is to know when to stop.   [ANTHONY *does not answer.*

WANKLIN. [*Very gravely.*] This way disaster lies. The ancient Trojans were fools to your father, Mrs. Underwood.   [*He goes out through the double doors.*

ENID. I want to speak to father, Frank.

>   [UNDERWOOD *follows* WANKLIN *out.* TENCH,
>   *passing round the table, is restoring order to
>   the scattered pens and papers.*

ENID. Aren't you coming, Dad?

>   [ANTHONY *shakes his head.* ENID *looks mean-
>   ingly at* TENCH.

ENID. Won't you go and have some lunch, Mr. Tench?

TENCH. [*With papers in his hand.*] Thank you, ma'am, thank you!   [*He goes slowly, looking back.*

ENID. [*Shutting the doors.*] I *do* hope it's settled, father!

ANTHONY. No!

ENID. [*Very disappointed.*] Oh! Haven't you done anything?   [ANTHONY *shakes his head.*

ENID. Frank says they all want to come to a compromise, really, except that man Roberts.

ANTHONY. *I* don't.

ENID. It's such a horrid position for us. If you were the wife of the manager, and lived down here, and saw it all. You can't realise, Dad!

ANTHONY. Indeed?

ENID. We see *all* the distress. *You* remember my maid Annie, who married Roberts? [ANTHONY *nods.*] It's so wretched, her heart's weak; since the strike began, she hasn't even been getting proper food. I know it for a fact, father.

ANTHONY. Give her what she wants, poor woman!

ENID. Roberts won't let her take anything from *us*.

ANTHONY. [*Staring before him.*] I can't be answerable for the men's obstinacy.

ENID. They're all suffering. Father! Do stop it, for my sake!

ANTHONY. [*With a keen look at her.*] You don't understand, my dear.

ENID. If I were on the board, I'd do something.

ANTHONY. What would you do?

ENID. It's because you can't bear to give way. It's so——

ANTHONY. Well?

ENID. So unnecessary.

ANTHONY. What do *you* know about necessity? Read your novels, play your music, talk your talk, but don't try and tell *me* what's at the bottom of a struggle like this.

ENID. I live down here, and see it.

ANTHONY. What d'you imagine stands between you and your class and these men that you're so sorry for?

ENID. [*Coldly.*] I don't know what you mean, father.

ANTHONY. In a few years you and your children would be down in the condition they're in, but for those who have the eyes to see things as they are and the backbone to stand up for themselves.

ENID. You don't know the state the men are in.

ANTHONY. I know it well enough.

ENID. You don't father; if you did, you wouldn't——

ANTHONY. It's you who don't know the simple facts of the position. What sort of mercy do you suppose you'd get if no one stood between you and the continual demands of labour? This sort of mercy—[*he puts his hand up to his throat and squeezes it.*] First would go your sentiments, my dear; then your culture, and your comforts would be going all the time!

ENID. I don't believe in barriers between classes.

ANTHONY. You—don't—believe—in—barriers—between the classes?

ENID. [*Coldly.*] And I don't know what that has to do with this question.

ANTHONY. It will take a generation or two for you to understand.

ENID. It's only you and Roberts, father, and you know it!   [ANTHONY *thrusts out his lower lip.*] It'll ruin the Company.

ANTHONY. Allow me to judge of that.

ENID. [*Resentfully.*] I won't stand by and let poor Annie Roberts suffer like this! And think of the children, father! I warn you.

ANTHONY. [*With a grim smile.*] What do you propose to do?

ENID. That's my affair.

[ANTHONY *only looks at her.*

ENID. [*In a changed voice, stroking his sleeve.*] Father,

you *know* you oughtn't to have this strain on you—
you know what Dr. Fisher said !

ANTHONY. No old man can afford to listen to old
women.

ENID. But you *have* done enough, even if it really
is such a matter of principle with you.

ANTHONY. You think so ?

ENID. Don't, Dad ! [*Her face works.*] You—you
might think of *us !*

ANTHONY. I am.

ENID. It'll break you down.

ANTHONY. [*Slowly.*] My dear, I am not going to
funk ; on that you may rely.

> [*Re-enter* TENCH *with papers ; he glances at them,
> then plucking up courage.*

TENCH. Beg pardon, Madam, I think I'd rather see
these papers were disposed of before I get my lunch.

> [ENID, *after an impatient glance at him, looks at
> her father, turns suddenly, and goes into the
> drawing-room.*

TENCH. [*Holding the papers and a pen to* ANTHONY,
very nervously.] Would you sign these for me, please
sir ?   [ANTHONY *takes the pen and signs.*

TENCH. [*Standing with a sheet of blotting-paper behind*
EDGAR's *chair, begins speaking nervously.*] I owe my
position to you, sir.

ANTHONY. Well ?

TENCH. I'm obliged to see everything that's going
on, sir ; I—I depend upon the Company entirely.
If anything were to happen to it, it'd be disastrous

for me. [ANTHONY *nods*.] And, of course, my wife's just had another; and so it makes me doubly anxious just now. And the rates are really terrible down our way.

ANTHONY. [*With grim amusement*.] Not more terrible than they are up mine.

TENCH. No, sir? [*Very nervously*.] I know the Company means a great deal to you, sir.

ANTHONY. It does; I founded it.

TENCH. Yes, sir. If the strike goes on it'll be very serious. I think the Directors are beginning to realise that, sir.

ANTHONY. [*Ironically*.] Indeed?

TENCH. I know you hold very strong views, sir, and it's always your habit to look things in the face; but I don't think the Directors—like it, sir, now they—they see it.

ANTHONY. [*Grimly*.] Nor you, it seems.

TENCH. [*With the ghost of a smile*.] No, sir; of course I've got my children, and my wife's delicate; in my position I *have* to think of these things. [ANTHONY *nods*.] It wasn't *that* I was going to say, sir, if you'll excuse me [*hesitates*]——

ANTHONY. Out with it, then!

TENCH. I know—from my own father, sir, that when you get on in life you do feel things dreadfully——

ANTHONY. [*Almost paternally*.] Come, out with it, Tench!

TENCH. I don't *like* to say it, sir.

ANTHONY. [*Stonily.*] You must.

TENCH. [*After a pause, desperately bolting it out.*] I think the Directors are going to throw you over, sir.

ANTHONY. [*Sits in silence.*] Ring the bell !

    [TENCH *nervously rings the bell and stands by the fire.*

TENCH. Excuse me saying such a thing. I was *only* thinking of you, sir.

    [FROST *enters from the hall, he comes to the foot of the table, and looks at* ANTHONY ; TENCH *covers his nervousness by arranging papers.*

ANTHONY. Bring me a whiskey and soda.

FROST. Anything to eat, sir ?

    [ANTHONY *shakes his head*—FROST *goes to the sideboard, and prepares the drink.*

TENCH. [*In a low voice, almost supplicating.*] If you *could* see your way, sir, it would be a great relief to my mind, it would indeed. [*He looks up at* ANTHONY, *who has not moved.*] It does make me so very anxious. I haven't slept properly for weeks, sir, and that's a fact.

    [ANTHONY *looks in his face, then slowly shakes his head.*

TENCH. [*Disheartened.*] No, sir ? [*He goes on arranging papers.* FROST *places the whiskey and soda on a salver and puts it down by* ANTHONY's *right hand. He stands away, looking gravely at* ANTHONY.

FROST. *Nothing* I can get you, sir?

> [ANTHONY *shakes his head.*]

You're aware, sir, of what the doctor said, sir?

ANTHONY. I am.

> [*A pause. FROST suddenly moves closer to him, and speaks in a low voice.*

FROST. This strike, sir; puttin' all this strain on you. Excuse me, sir, is it—is it worth it, sir?

> [ANTHONY *mutters some words that are inaudible.*]

Very good, sir!

> [*He turns and goes out into the hall—*TENCH *makes two attempts to speak; but meeting his chairman's gaze he drops his eyes, and turning dismally, he too goes out. ANTHONY is left alone. He grips the glass, tilts it, and drinks deeply; then sets it down with a deep and rumbling sigh, and leans back in his chair.*

> *The curtain falls.*

ACT II

SCENE I

[*It is half-past three. In the kitchen of Roberts' cottage a meagre little fire is burning. The room is clean and tidy, very barely furnished, with a brick floor and white-washed walls, much stained with smoke. There is a kettle on the fire. A door opposite the fireplace opens inwards from a snowy street. On the wooden table are a cup and saucer, a teapot, knife, and plate of bread and cheese. Close to the fireplace in an old armchair, wrapped in a rug, sits* MRS. ROBERTS, *a thin and dark-haired woman about thirty-five, with patient eyes. Her hair is not done up, but tied back with a piece of ribbon. By the fire, too, is* MRS. YEO; *a red-haired, broad-faced person. Sitting near the table is* MRS. ROUS, *an old lady, ashen-white, with silver hair; by the door, standing, as if about to go, is* MRS. BULGIN, *a little pale, pinched-up woman. In a chair, with her elbows resting on the table, and her face resting in her hands sits* MADGE THOMAS, *a good-looking girl, of twenty-two, with high cheekbones, deep-set eyes, and dark, untidy hair. She is listening to the talk but she neither speaks nor moves.*

223

Mrs. Yeo. So he give me a sixpence, and that's the first bit o' money *I* seen this week. There an't much 'eat to this fire. Come and warm yerself, Mrs. Rous, you're lookin' as white as the snow, you are.

Mrs. Rous. [*Shivering—placidly.*] Ah! but the winter my old man was took was the proper winter. Seventy-nine that was, when none of you was hardly born—not Madge Thomas, nor Sue Bulgin. [*Looking at them in turn.*] Annie Roberts, 'ow old were you dear?

Mrs. Roberts. Seven, Mrs. Rous.

Mrs. Rous. Seven—well ther'! A tiny little thing!

Mrs. Yeo. [*Aggressively.*] Well, I was ten myself, *I* remembers it.

Mrs. Rous. [*Placidly.*] The Company hadn't been started three years. Father was workin' on the acid that's 'ow he got 'is pisoned leg. I kep' sayin' to 'im "Father, you've got a pisoned leg." "Well," 'e, said, "Mother, pison or no pison, I can't afford to go a-layin' up." An' two days after he was on 'is back, and never got up again. It was Providence! There wasn't none o' these Compension Acts then.

Mrs. Yeo. Ye hadn't no strike that winter! [*With grim humour.*] This winter's 'ard enough for me. Mrs. Roberts, you don't want no 'arder winter, do you? Wouldn't seem natural to 'ave a dinner, would it, Mrs. Bulgin?

Mrs. Bulgin. We've had bread and tea last four days.

Mrs. Yeo. You got that Friday's laundry job?

MRS. BULGIN. [*Dispiritedly.*] They said they'd give it me, but when I went last Friday, they were full up. I got to go again next week.

MRS. YEO. Ah! There's too many after that. I send Yeo out on the ice to put on the gentry's skates an' pick up what 'e can. Stops 'im from broodin' about the 'ouse.

MRS. BULGIN. [*In a desolate, matter-of-fact voice.*] Leavin' out the men—it's bad enough with the children. I keep 'em in bed, they don't get so hungry when they're not running about; but they're that restless in bed they worry your life out.

MRS. YEO. You're lucky they're all so small. It's the goin' to school that makes 'em 'ungry. Don't Bulgin give you *any*thin'?

MRS. BULGIN. [*Shakes her head, then, as though by afterthought.*] Would if he could, I s'pose.

MRS. YEO. [*Sardonically.*] What! 'Aven't 'e got no shares in the Company?

MRS. ROUS. [*Rising with tremulous cheerfulness.*] Well, good-bye, Annie Roberts, I'm going along home.

MRS. ROBERTS. Stay an' have a cup of tea, Mrs. Rous?

MRS. ROUS. [*With the faintest smile.*] Roberts'll want 'is tea when he comes in. I'll just go an' get to bed; it's warmer there than anywhere.

[*She moves very shakily towards the door.*

MRS. YEO. [*Rising and giving her an arm.*] Come on, Mother, take my arm; we're all going' the same way.

P

Mrs. Rous. [*Taking the arm.*] Thank you, my dearies!   [They *go out, followed by* Mrs. Bulgin.

Madge. [*Moving for the first time.*] There, Annie, you see that! I told George Rous, "Don't think to have my company till you've made an end of all this trouble. You ought to be ashamed," I said, "with your own mother looking like a ghost, and not a stick to put on the fire. So long as you're able to fill your pipes, you'll let us starve." "I'll take my oath, Madge," he said," "I've not had smoke nor drink these three weeks!" "Well, then, why do you go on with it?" "I can't go back on Roberts!" . . . That's it! Roberts, always Roberts! They'd all drop it but for him. When *he* talks it's the devil that comes into them.

[*A silence.* Mrs. Roberts *makes a movement of pain.*] Ah! *You* don't want him beaten! He's your man. With everybody like their own shadows! [*She makes a gesture towards* Mrs. Roberts.] If Rous wants me he must give up Roberts. If *he* gave him up—they all would. They're only waiting for a lead. Father's against him—they're all against him in their hearts.

Mrs. Roberts. You won't beat Roberts! [They *look silently at each other.*]

Madge. Won't I? The cowards—when their own mothers and their own children don't know where to turn.

Mrs. Roberts. Madge!

Madge. [*Looking searchingly at* Mrs. Roberts.] I

wonder he can look *you* in the face. [*She squats before
the fire, with her hands out to the flame.*] Harness is here
again.   They'll have to make up their minds to-day.

MRS. ROBERTS. [*In a soft, slow voice, with a slight
West-country burr.*] Roberts will never give up the
furnacemen and engineers.   'Twouldn't be right.

MADGE. You can't deceive me.   It's just his pride.

> [*A tapping at the door is heard, the women turn
> as* ENID *enters.   She wears a round fur cap,
> and a jacket of squirrel's fur.   She closes the
> door behind her.*

ENID. Can I come in, Annie?

MRS. ROBERTS. [*Flinching.*] Miss Enid !   Give Mrs.
Underwood a chair, Madge !

> [MADGE *gives* ENID *the chair she has been sitting on.*

ENID. Thank you !

ENID. Are you any better?

MRS. ROBERTS. Yes, M'm ; thank you, M'm.

ENID. [*Looking at the sullen* MADGE *as though request-
ing her departure.*] Why did you send back the jelly ?
I call that really wicked of you !

MRS. ROBERTS. Thank you, M'm, I'd no need
for it.

ENID. Of course !   It was Roberts' doing, wasn't
it ?   How can he let all this suffering go on amongst
you ?

MADGE. [*Suddenly.*] What suffering ?

ENID. [*Surprised.*] I beg your pardon !

MADGE. Who said there was suffering ?

MRS. ROBERTS. Madge !

MADGE. [*Throwing her shawl over her head.*] Please to let us keep ourselves to ourselves.   We don't want you coming here and spying on us.

ENID. [*Confronting her, but without rising.*] I didn't speak to *you*.

MADGE. [*In a low, fierce voice.*] Keep your kind feelings to yourself.   You think you can come amongst us, but you're mistaken.   Go back and tell the Manager that.

ENID. [*Stonily.*] This is not your house.

MADGE. [*Turning to the door.*] No, it is not my house ; keep clear of my house, Mrs. Underwood.

[*She goes out.   ENID taps her fingers on the table.*

MRS. ROBERTS. Please to forgive Madge Thomas, M'm ; she's a bit upset to-day.   [*A pause.*

ENID. [*Looking at her.*] Oh, I think they're so *stupid*, all of them.

MRS. ROBERTS. [*With a faint smile.*] Yes, M'm.

ENID. Is Roberts out ?

MRS. ROBERTS. Yes, M'm.

ENID. It is *his doing*, that they don't come to an agreement.   Now isn't it, Annie ?

MRS. ROBERTS. [*Softly, with her eyes on ENID, and moving the fingers of one hand continually on her breast.*] They do say that your father, M'm——

ENID. My father's getting an old man, and you know what old men are.

MRS. ROBERTS. I am sorry, M'm.

ENID. [*More softly.*] I don't expect *you* to feel sorry, Annie.   I know it's his fault as well as Roberts'.

MRS. ROBERTS. I'm sorry for any one that gets old, M'm; it's dreadful to get old, and Mr. Anthony was such a fine old man I always used to think.

ENID. [*Impulsively.*] He always liked you, don't you remember? Look here, Annie, what can I do? I do so want to know. You don't get what you ought to have. [*Going to the fire, she takes the kettle off, and looks for coals.*] And you're so naughty sending back the soup and things!

MRS. ROBERTS. [*With a faint smile.*] Yes, M'm?

ENID. [*Resentfully.*] Why, you haven't even got coals?

MRS. ROBERTS. If you please, M'm, to put the kettle on again; Roberts won't have long for his tea when he comes in. He's got to meet the men at four.

ENID. [*Putting the kettle on.*] That means he'll lash them into a fury again. Can't you stop his going, Annie? [MRS. ROBERTS *smiles ironically.*] Have you tried? [*A silence.*] Does he know how ill you are?

MRS. ROBERTS. It's only my weak 'eart, M'm.

ENID. You used to be so well when you were with us.

MRS. ROBERTS. [*Stiffening.*] Roberts is always good to me.

ENID. But you ought to have everything you want, and you have nothing!

MRS. ROBERTS. [*Appealingly.*] They tell me I don't look like a dyin' woman?

ENID. Of course you don't; if you could only have

proper—— Will you see my doctor if I send him to you? I'm sure he'd do you good.

MRS. ROBERTS. [*With faint questioning.*] Yes, M'm.

ENID. Madge Thomas oughtn't to come here; she only excites you. As if I didn't know what suffering there is amongst the men! I do feel for them dreadfully, but you know they *have* gone too far.

MRS. ROBERTS. [*Continually moving her fingers.*] They say there's no other way to get better wages, M'm.

ENID. [*Earnestly.*] But, Annie, that's why the Union won't help them. My husband's very sympathetic with the men, but he says they're not underpaid.

MRS. ROBERTS. No, M'm?

ENID. They never think how the Company could go on if we paid the wages they want.

MRS. ROBERTS. [*With an effort.*] But the dividends having been so big, M'm.

ENID. [*Taken aback.*] You all seem to think the shareholders are rich men, but they're not—most of them are really no better off than working men. [MRS. ROBERTS *smiles.*] They have to keep up appearances.

MRS. ROBERTS. Yes, M'm?

ENID. You don't have to pay rates and taxes, and a hundred other things that they do. If the men didn't spend such a lot in drink and betting they'd be quite well off!

MRS. ROBERTS. They say, workin' so hard, they must have some pleasure.

ENID. But surely not low pleasure like that.

MRS. ROBERTS. [*A little resentfully.*] Roberts never touches a drop ; and he's never had a bet in his life.

ENID. Oh ! but he's not a com—— I mean he's an engineer—a superior man.

MRS. ROBERTS. Yes, M'm. Roberts says they've no chance of other pleasures.

ENID. [*Musing.*] Of course, I know it's hard.

MRS. ROBERTS. [*With a spice of malice.*] And they say gentlefolk's just as bad.

ENID. [*With a smile.*] I go as far as most people, Annie, but you know, yourself, that's nonsense.

MRS. ROBERTS. [*With painful effort.*] A lot o' the men never go near the Public ; but even they don't save but very little, and that goes if there's illness.

ENID. But they've got their clubs, haven't they ?

MRS. ROBERTS. The clubs only give up to eighteen shillin's a week, M'm, and it's not much amongst a family. Roberts says workin' folk have always lived from hand to mouth. Sixpence to-day is worth more than a shillin' to-morrow, that's what they say.

ENID. But that's the spirit of gambling.

MRS. ROBERTS. [*With a sort of excitement.*] Roberts says a working man's life is all a gamble, from the time 'e's born to the time 'e dies.

> [ENID *leans forward, interested.* MRS. ROBERTS
> *goes on with a growing excitement that culmin-*
> *ates in the personal feeling of the last words.*]

He says, M'm, that when a working man's baby is born, it's a toss-up from breath to breath whether it ever draws another, and so on all 'is life; an' when he comes to be old, it's the workhouse or the grave. He says that without a man is very near, and pinches and stints 'imself and 'is children to save, there can't be neither surplus nor security. That's why he wouldn't have no children [*she sinks back*], not though I *wanted* them.

ENID. Yes, yes, I know!

MRS. ROBERTS. No you don't, M'm. You've got your children, and you'll never need to trouble for them.

ENID. [*Gently.*] You oughtn't to be talking so much, Annie. [*Then, in spite of herself.*] But Roberts was paid a lot of money, wasn't he, for discovering that process?

MRS. ROBERTS. [*On the defensive.*] All Roberts' savin's have gone. He's always looked forward to this strike. He says he's no right to a farthing when the others are suffering. 'Tisn't so with all o' them! Some don't seem to care no more than that—so long as they get their own.

ENID. I don't see how they can be expected to when they're suffering like this. [*In a changed voice.*] But Roberts ought to think of *you!* It's all terrible! The kettle's boiling. Shall I make the tea? [*She takes the teapot, and seeing tea there, pours water into it.*] Won't you have a cup?

MRS. ROBERTS. No, thank you, M'm. [*She is*

listening, as though for footsteps.] I'd sooner you didn't see Roberts, M'm, he gets so wild.

ENID. Oh! but I must, Annie; I'll be quite calm, I promise.

MRS. ROBERTS. It's life an' death to him, M'm.

ENID. [*Very gently.*] I'll get him to talk to me outside, we won't excite you.

MRS. ROBERTS. [*Faintly.*] No, M'm.

> [*She gives a violent start. ROBERTS has come in, unseen.*

ROBERTS. [*Removing his hat—with subtle mockery.*] Beg pardon for coming in; you're engaged with a lady, I see.

ENID. Can I speak to you, Mr. Roberts?

ROBERTS. Whom have I the pleasure of addressing, Ma'am?

ENID. But surely you know me! I'm Mrs. Underwood.

ROBERTS. [*With a bow of malice.*] The daughter of our chairman.

ENID. [*Earnestly.*] I've come on purpose to speak to you; will you come outside a minute?

> [*She looks at MRS. ROBERTS.*

ROBERTS. [*Hanging up his hat.*] I have nothing to say, Ma'am.

ENID. But I *must* speak to you, please.

> [*She moves towards the door.*

ROBERTS. [*With sudden venom.*] I have not the time to listen!

MRS. ROBERTS. David!

ENID. Mr. Roberts, *please !*

ROBERTS. [*Taking off his overcoat.*] I am sorry to disoblige a lady—Mr. Anthony's daughter.

ENID. [*Wavering, then with sudden decision.*] Mr. Roberts, I know you've another meeting of the men.

[ROBERTS *bows.*]

I came to appeal to you. Please, please try to come to some compromise ; give way a little, if it's only for your own sakes !

ROBERTS. [*Speaking to himself.*] The daughter of Mr. Anthony begs me to give way a little, if it's for our own sakes.

ENID. For everybody's sake ; for your wife's sake.

ROBERTS. For my wife's sake, for everybody's sake —for the sake of Mr. Anthony.

ENID. Why are you so bitter against my father ? He has never done anything to you.

ROBERTS. Has he not ?

ENID. He can't help his views, any more than you can help yours.

ROBERTS. I really didn't know that I had a right to views !

ENID. He's an old man, and you——

[*Seeing his eyes fixed on her, she stops.*

ROBERTS. [*Without raising his voice.*] If I saw Mr. Anthony going to die, and I could save him by lifting my hand, I would not lift the little finger of it.

ENID. You—you—   [*She stops again biting her lips.*

ROBERTS. I would not, and that's flat '

ENID. [*Coldly.*] You don't mean what you say, and you know it!

ROBERTS. I mean every word of it.

ENID. But why?

ROBERTS. [*With a flash.*] Mr. Anthony stands for tyranny! That's why!

ENID. Nonsense!

> [MRS. ROBERTS *makes a movement as if to rise, but sinks back in her chair.*

ENID. [*With an impetuous movement.*] Annie!

ROBERTS. Please not to touch my wife!

ENID. [*Recoiling with a sort of horror.*] I believe— you are mad.

ROBERTS. The house of a madman then is not the fit place for a lady.

ENID. I'm not afraid of you.

ROBERTS. [*Bowing.*] I would not expect the daughter of Mr. Anthony to be afraid. Mr. Anthony is not a coward like the rest of them.

ENID. [*Suddenly.*] I suppose you think it brave, then, to go on with this struggle.

ROBERTS. Does Mr. Anthony think it brave to fight against women and children? Mr. Anthony is a rich man, I believe; does he think it brave to fight against those who haven't a penny? Does he think it brave to set children crying with hunger, an' women shivering with cold?

ENID. [*Putting up her hand, as though warding off a blow.*] My father is acting on his principles, and you know it!

ROBERTS. And so am I!

ENID. You hate us; and you can't bear to be beaten!

ROBERTS. Neither can Mr. Anthony, for all that he may say.

ENID. At any rate you might have pity on your wife.

> [MRS. ROBERTS *who has her hand pressed to her heart, takes it away, and tries to calm her breathing.*

ROBERTS. Madam, I have no more to say.

> [*He takes up the loaf. There is a knock at the door, and* UNDERWOOD *comes in. He stands looking at them,* ENID *turns to him, then seems undecided.*

UNDERWOOD. Enid!

ROBERTS. [*Ironically.*] Ye were not needing to come for your wife, Mr. Underwood. We are not rowdies.

UNDERWOOD. I know that, Roberts. I hope Mrs. Roberts is better.

> [ROBERTS *turns away without answering.*]

Come, Enid!

ENID. I make one more appeal to you, Mr. Roberts, for the sake of your wife.

ROBERTS. [*With polite malice.*] If I might advise ye, Ma'am—make it for the sake of your husband and your father.

> [ENID, *suppressing a retort, goes out.* UNDER-WOOD *opens the door for her and follows.* ROBERTS, *going to the fire, holds out his hands to the dying glow.*

ROBERTS. How goes it, my girl? Feeling better, are you?

[MRS. ROBERTS *smiles faintly. He brings his overcoat and wraps it round her.*]

[*Looking at his watch.*] Ten minutes to four! [*As though inspired.*] I've seen their faces, there's no fight in them, except for that one old robber.

MRS. ROBERTS. Won't you stop and eat, David? You've 'ad nothing all day!

ROBERTS. [*Putting his hand to his throat.*] Can't swallow till those old sharks are out o' the town. [*He walks up and down.*] I shall have a bother with the men—there's no heart in them, the cowards. Blind as bats, they are—can't see a day before their noses.

MRS. ROBERTS. It's the women, David.

ROBERTS. Ah! So they say! They can remember the women when their own bellies speak! The women never stops them from the drink; but from a little suffering to themselves in a sacred cause, the women stop them fast enough.

MRS. ROBERTS. But think o' the children, David.

ROBERTS. Ah! If they will go breeding themselves for slaves, without a thought o' the future o' them they breed——

MRS. ROBERTS. [*Gasping.*] That's enough, David; don't begin to talk of that—I won't—I can't——

ROBERTS. [*Staring at her.*] Now, now, my girl!

MRS. ROBERTS. [*Breathlessly.*] No, no, David—I won't!

ROBERTS. There, there! Come, come! That's right! [*Bitterly.*] Not one penny will they put by for a day like this. Not they! Hand to mouth—Gad!—I know them! They've broke my heart. There was no holdin' them at the start, but now the pinch 'as come.

MRS. ROBERTS. How can you expect it, David? They're not made of iron.

ROBERTS. Expect it? Wouldn't I expect what I would do meself? Wouldn't I starve an' rot rather than give in? What one man can do, another can.

MRS. ROBERTS. And the women?

ROBERTS. This is not women's work.

MRS. ROBERTS. [*With a flash of malice.*] No, the women may die for all you care. That's their work.

ROBERTS. [*Averting his eyes.*] Who talks of dying? No one will die till we have beaten these——

> [*He meets her eyes again, and again turns his away. Excitedly.*]

This is what I've been waiting for all these months. To get the old robbers down, and send them home again without a farthin's worth o' change. I've seen their faces, I tell you, in the valley of the shadow of defeat.   [*He goes to the peg and takes down his hat.*

MRS. ROBERTS. [*Following with her eyes—softly.*] Take your overcoat, David; it must be bitter cold.

ROBERTS. [*Coming up to her—his eyes are furtive.*] No, no! There, there, stay quiet and warm. I won't be long, my girl.

MRS. ROBERTS. [*With soft bitterness.*] You'd better take it.

> [*She lifts the coat. But* ROBERTS *puts it back, and wraps it round her. He tries to meet her eyes, but cannot.* MRS. ROBERTS *stays huddled in the coat, her eyes, that follow him about, are half malicious, half yearning. He looks at his watch again, and turns to go. In the doorway he meets* JAN THOMAS, *a boy of ten in clothes too big for him, carrying a penny whistle.*

ROBERTS. Hallo, boy !

> [*He goes,* JAN *stops within a yard of* MRS. ROBERTS, *and stares at her without a word.*

MRS. ROBERTS. Well, Jan !

JAN. Father's coming ; sister Madge is coming.

> [*He sits at the table, and fidgets with his whistle ; he blows three vague notes ; then imitates a cuckoo.*

> [*There is a tap on the door.* OLD THOMAS *comes in.*

THOMAS. A very coot tay to you, Ma'am. It is petter that you are.

MRS. ROBERTS. Thank you, Mr. Thomas.

THOMAS. [*Nervously.*] Roberts in ?

MRS. ROBERTS. Just gone on to the meeting, Mr. Thomas.

THOMAS. [*With relief, becoming talkative.*] This is fery unfortunate, look you ! I came to tell him that we must make terms with London. It [is a fery great pity he is gone to the meeting. He will be kicking against the pricks, I am thinking.

Mrs. Roberts. [*Half rising.*] He'll never give in, Mr. Thomas.

Thomas. You must not be fretting, that is very pat for you. Look you, there iss hartly any mans for supporting him now, but the engineers and George Rous. [*Solemnly.*] This strike is no longer coing with Chapel, look you! I have listened carefully, an' I have talked with her. [Jan *blows.*] Sst! I don't care what th' others say, I say that *Chapel means us* to be stopping the trouple, that is what I make of her; and it is my opinion that this is the fery best thing for all of us. If it wasn't my opinion, I ton't say— but it is my opinion, look you.

Mrs. Roberts. [*Trying to suppress her excitement.*] I don't know what'll come to Roberts, if you give in.

Thomas. It iss no disgrace whateffer! All that a mortal man coult do he hass tone. It iss against Human Nature he hass gone; fery natural—any man may to that; but Chapel has spoken and he must not co against *her.* [Jan *imitates the cuckoo.* Ton't make that squeaking! [*Going to the door.*] Here iss my taughter come to sit with you. A fery goot day, Ma'am—no fretting—rememper!

[Madge *comes in and stands at the open door, watching the street.*

Madge. You'll be late, Father; they're beginning.

[*She catches him by the sleeve.*] For the love of God,
stand up to him, Father—this time!

THOMAS. [*Detaching his sleeve with dignity.*] Leave
me to do what's proper, girl!

> [*He goes out,* MADGE, *in the centre of the open
> doorway, slowly moves in, as though before
> the approach of some one.*

ROUS. [*Appearing in the doorway.*] Madge!

> [MADGE *stands with her back to* MRS. ROBERTS,
> *staring at him with her head up and her
> hands behind her.*

ROUS. [*Who has a fierce distracted look.*] Madge!
I'm going to the meeting.

> [MADGE, *without moving, smiles contemptuously.*]
D'ye hear me?   [*They speak in quick low voices.*

MADGE. I hear! Go, and kill your own Mother,
if you must.

> [ROUS *seizes her by both her arms. She stands
> rigid, with her head bent back. He releases
> her, and he too stands motionless.*

ROUS. I swore to stand by Roberts. I swore that!
Ye want me to go back on what I've sworn.

MADGE. [*With slow soft mockery.*] You are a pretty
lover!

ROUS. Madge!

MADGE. [*Smiling.*] I've heard that lovers do what
their girls ask them—[JAN *sounds the cuckoo's notes*]—
but that's not true, it seems!

ROUS. You'd make a blackleg of me!

MADGE. [*With her eyes half-closed.*] Do it for me!

Q

Rous. [*Dashing his hand across his brow.*] Damn! I
can't!

Madge. [*Swiftly.*] Do it for me!

Rous. [*Through his teeth.*] Don't play the wanton
with me!

Madge. [*With a movement of her hand towards* Jan
—*quick and low.*] I would be *that* for the children's
sake!

Rous, [*In a fierce whisper.*] Madge! Oh, Madge!

Madge. [*With soft mockery.*] But *you* can't break
your word for me!

Rous. [*With a choke.*] Then, Begod, I can!

[*He turns and rushes off.*

[Madge *stands with a faint smile on her face,
    looking after him.   She turns to* Mrs.
    Roberts.

Madge. I have done for Roberts!

Mrs. Roberts. [*Scornfully.*] Done for my man,
with that—— !   [*She sinks back.*

Madge. [*running to her, and feeling her hands.*]
You're as cold as a stone! You want a drop of
brandy. Jan, run to the "Lion"; say, I sent you
for Mrs. Roberts.

Mrs. Roberts. [*With a feeble movement.*] I'll just
sit quiet, Madge. Give Jan—his—tea.

Madge. [*Giving* Jan *a slice of bread.*] There, ye little
rascal. Hold your piping. [*Going to the fire, she
kneels.*] It's going out.

Mrs. Roberts. [*With a faint smile.*] 'Tis all the
same!   [Jan *begins to blow his whistle.*

MADGE. Tsht! Tsht!—you——   [JAN *stops*.

MRS. ROBERTS. [*Smiling.*] Let 'im play, Madge.

MADGE. [*On her knees at the fire, listening.*] Waiting an' waiting. I've no patience with it; waiting an' waiting—that's what a woman has to do! Can you hear them at it—I can!

> [JAN *begins again to play his whistle;* MADGE *gets up; half tenderly she ruffles his hair; then, sitting, leans her elbows on the table, and her chin on her hands. Behind her, on* MRS. ROBERTS' *face the smile has changed to horrified surprise. She makes a sudden movement, sitting forward, pressing her hands against her breast. Then slowly she sinks back; slowly her face loses the look of pain, the smile returns. She fixes her eyes again on* JAN, *and moves her lips and finger to the tune.*

The curtain falls.

SCENE II

*[It is past four.   In a grey, failing light, an open muddy
space is crowded with workmen.   Beyond, divided from
it by a barbed-wire fence, is the raised towing-path of
a canal, on which is moored a barge.   In the dis-
tance are marshes and snow-covered hills.   The
" Works' " high wall runs from the canal across the
open space, and in the angle of this wall is a rude
platform of barrels and boards.   On it, HARNESS is
standing.   ROBERTS, a little apart from the crowd,
leans his back against the wall.   On the raised towing-
path two bargemen lounge and smoke indifferently.*

HARNESS. [*Holding out his hand.*] Well, I've spoken
to you straight.   If I speak till to-morrow I can't
say more.

JAGO. [*A dark, sallow, Spanish-looking man with a
short, thin beard.*] Mister, want to ask you!   Can
they get blacklegs?

BULGIN. [*Menacing.*] Let 'em try.

[*There are savage murmurs from the crowd.*

BROWN. [*A round-faced man.*] Where could they
get 'em then?

EVANS. [*A small, restless, harassed man, with a fighting
face.*]   There's always blacklegs; it's the nature of
'em. There's always men that'll save their own skins.

[*Another savage murmur.   There is a movement,
and old THOMAS, joining the crowd, takes
his stand in front.*

HARNESS. [*Holding up his hand.*] They can't get
them. But that won't help you. Now men, be
reasonable. Your demands would have brought on
us the burden of a dozen strikes at a time when we
were not prepared for them. The Unions live by
Justice, not to one, but all. Any fair man will tell
you—you were ill-advised ! I don't say you go too
far for that which you're entitled to, but you're going
too far for the moment ; you've dug a pit for yourselves. Are you to stay there, or are you to climb
out ? Come !

LEWIS. [*A clean-cut Welshman with a dark moustache.*]
You've hit it, Mister ! Which is it to be ?

> [*Another movement in the crowd, and* ROUS,
> *coming quickly, takes his stand next* THOMAS.

HARNESS. Cut your demands to the right pattern,
and we'll see you through ; refuse, and don't expect
me to waste my time coming down here again. I'm
not the sort that speaks at random, as you ought to
know by this time. If you're the sound men I take
you for—no matter who advises you against it—[*he
fixes his eyes on* ROBERTS] you'll make up your minds
to come in, and trust to us to get your terms. Which
is it to be ? Hands together, and victory—or—the
starvation you've got now ?

> [*A prolonged murmur from the crowd.*

JAGO. [*Sullenly.*] Talk about what you know.

HARNESS. [*Lifting his voice above the murmur.*] Know?
[*With cold passion.*] All that you've been through, my
friend, I've been through—I was through it when I

was no bigger than [*pointing to a youth*] that shaver there; the Unions then weren't what they are now. What's made them strong? It's hands together that's made them strong. I've been through it all, I tell you, the brand's on my soul yet. I know what you've suffered—there's nothing you can tell me that I don't know; but the whole is greater than the part, and you are only the part. Stand by us, and we will stand by you.

> [*Quartering them with his eyes, he waits. The murmuring swells; the men form little groups.* GREEN, BULGIN, *and* LEWIS *talk together.*

LEWIS. Speaks very sensible, the Union chap.

GREEN. [*Quietly.*] Ah! if I'd a been *listened* to, you'd 'ave 'eard sense these two months past.

> [*The bargemen are seen laughing.*

LEWIS. [*Pointing.*] Look at those two blanks over the fence there!

BULGIN. [*With gloomy violence.*] They'd best stop their cackle, or I'll break their jaws.

JAGO. [*Suddenly.*] You say the furnace men's paid enough?

HARNESS. I did not say they were paid enough; I said they were paid as much as the furnace men in similar works elsewhere.

EVANS. That's a lie! [*Hubbub.*] What about Harper's?

HARNESS. [*With cold irony.*] You may look at home

for lies, my man.   Harper's shifts are longer, the
pay works out the same.

HENRY ROUS. [*A dark edition of his brother George.*]
Will ye support us in double pay overtime Satur-
days?

HARNESS. Yes, we will.

JAGO. What have ye done with our subscriptions?

HARNESS. [*Coldly.*] I have told you what we *will*
do with them.

EVANS. Ah! *will*, it's always will! Ye'd have our
mates desert us.   [*Hubbub.*

BULGIN. [*Shouting.*] Hold your row!

[EVANS *looks round angrily.*

HARNESS. [*Lifting his voice.*] Those who know their
right hands from their lefts know that the Unions
are neither thieves nor traitors.   I've said my say.
Figure it out my lads; when you want me you know
where I shall be.

> [*He jumps down, the crowd gives way, he passes
> through them, and goes away.   A* BARGEMAN
> *looks after him jerking his pipe with a de-
> risive gesture.   The men close up in groups,
> and many looks are cast at* ROBERTS, *who
> stands alone against the wall.*

EVANS. He wants ye to turn blacklegs, that's what
he wants.   He wants ye to go back on us.   Sooner
than turn blackleg—I'd starve, I would.

BULGIN. Who's talkin' o' blacklegs—mind what
you're saying, will you?

BLACKSMITH. [*A youth with yellow hair and huge arms.*] What about the women?

EVANS. They can stand what we can stand, I suppose, can't they?

BLACKSMITH. Ye've no wife?

EVANS. An' don't want one!

THOMAS. [*Raising his voice.*] Aye! Give us the power to come to terms with London, lads.

DAVIES. [*A dark, slow-fly, gloomy man.*] Go up the platform, if you got anything to say, go up an' say it.

> [*There are cries of " Thomas! "   He is pushed towards the platform ; he ascends it with difficulty, and bares his head, waiting for silence.   A hush!*

RED-HAIRED YOUTH. [*Suddenly.*] Coot old Thomas!

> [*A hoarse laugh ; the bargemen exchange remarks ; a hush again, and* THOMAS *begins speaking.*

THOMAS. We are all in the tepth together, and it iss Nature that has put us there.

HENRY ROUS. It's London put us there!

EVANS. It's the Union.

THOMAS. It iss not Lonton; nor it iss not the Union—it iss Nature. It iss no disgrace whateffer to a potty to give in to Nature. For this Nature iss a fery pig thing ; it is pigger than what a man is. There iss more years to my hett than to the hett of any one here. It is fery pat, look you, this coing against Nature. It is pat to make other potties suffer, when there is nothing to pe cot py it.

[*A laugh.* THOMAS *angrily goes on.*]
What are ye laughing at? It is pat, I say! We are fighting for a principle; there is nopotty that shall say I am not a peliever in principle. Putt when Nature says "No further," then it is no coot snapping your fingers in her face.

[*A laugh from* ROBERTS, *and murmurs of approval.*]
This Nature must pe humort. It is a man's pisiness to pe pure, honest, just and merciful. That's what Chapel tells you. [*To* ROBERTS, *angrily.*] And, look you, David Roberts, Chapel tells you ye can do that without coing against Nature.

JAGO. What about the Union?

THOMAS. I ton't trust the Union; they haf treated us like tirt. "Do what we tell you," said they. I haf peen captain of the furnace-men twenty years, and I say to the Union—[*excitedly*]—"Can you tell me then, as well as I can tell you, what iss the right wages for the work that these men do?" For fife and twenty years I haf paid my moneys to the Union and—[*with great excitement*]—for nothings! What iss that but roguery, for all that this Mr. Harness says!   [*Murmurs.*

EVANS. Hear, hear.

HENRY ROUS. Get on with you! Cut on with it then!

THOMAS. Look you, if a man toes not trust me, am I coing to trust him?

JAGO. That's right.

THOMAS. Let them alone for rogues, and act for ourselves.   [*Murmurs.*

BLACKSMITH. That's what we been doin', haven't we?

THOMAS. [*With increased excitement.*] I wass brought up to do for meself. I wass brought up to go without a thing, if I hat not moneys to puy it. There iss too much, look you, of doing things with other people's moneys. We haf fought fair, and if we haf peen peaten, it iss no fault of ours. Gif us the power to make terms with London for ourself; if we ton't succeed, I say it iss petter to take our peating like men, than to tie like togs, or hang on to others' coat-tails to make them do our pusiness for us!

EVANS. [*Muttering.*] Who wants to?

THOMAS. [*Craning.*] What's that? If I stand up to a potty, and he knocks me town, I am not to go hollering to other potties to help me; I am to stand up again; and if he knocks me town properly, I am to stay there, isn't that right?   [*Laughter.*

JAGO. No Union!

HENRY ROUS. Union!   [*Others take up the shout.*

EVANS. Blacklegs!

     [BULGIN *and the* BLACKSMITH *shake their fists*
          at EVANS.

THOMAS. [*With a gesture.*] I am an olt man, look you.   [*A sudden silence, then murmurs again.*

LEWIS. Olt fool, with his "No Union!"

BULGIN. Them furnace chaps! For twopence I'd
smash the faces o' the lot of them.

GREEN. If I'd 'a been listened to at the first——

THOMAS. [*Wiping his brow.*] I'm comin' now to what
I was coing to say——

DAVIES. [*Muttering.*] An' time too!

THOMAS. [*Solemnly.*] Chapel says: Ton't carry on
this strife! Put an end to it!

JAGO. That's a lie! Chapel says go on!

THOMAS. [*Scornfully.*] Inteet! I haf ears to my
head.

RED-HAIRED YOUTH. Ah! long ones!   [*A laugh.*

JAGO. Your ears have misbeled you then.

THOMAS. [*Excitedly.*] Ye cannot be right if I am, ye
cannot haf it both ways.

RED-HAIRED YOUTH. Chapel can though!

> [*"The Shaver" laughs; there are murmurs
> from the crowd.*

THOMAS. [*Fixing his eyes on "The Shaver."*] Ah!
ye're coing the roat to tamnation. An' so I say to
all of you. If ye co against Chapel I will not pe
with you, nor will any other Got-fearing man.

> [*He steps down from the platform. JAGO makes
> his way towards it. There are cries of
> "Don't let 'im go up!"*

JAGO. Don't let him go up? That's free speech,
that is. [*He goes up.*] I ain't got much to say to you.
Look at the matter plain; ye've come the road this
far, and now you want to chuck the journey. We've
all been in one boat; and now you want to pull in

two.   We engineers have stood by you; ye're ready
now, are ye, to give us the go-by?   If we'd a-known
that before, we'd not a-started out with you so early
one bright morning!   That's all I've got to say.   Old
man Thomas a'n't got his Bible lesson right.   If you
give up to London, or to Harness, now, it's givin' us
the chuck—to save your skins—you won't get over
that, my boys; it's a dirty thing to do.

> [*He gets down; during his little speech, which
> is ironically spoken, there is a restless dis-
> comfort in the crowd.   Rous, stepping for-
> ward, jumps on the platform.   He has an
> air of fierce distraction.   Sullen murmurs of
> disapproval from the crowd.*

Rous.   [*Speaking with great excitement.*]   I'm no blanky
orator, mates, but wot I say is drove from me.   What
I say is yuman nature.   Can a man set an' see 'is
mother starve?   Can 'e now?

Roberts.   [*Starting forward.*]   Rous!

Rous.   [*Staring at him fiercely.*]   Sim 'Arness said fair!
I've changed my mind!

Roberts.   Ah!   Turned your coat you mean!

> [*The crowd manifests a great surprise.*

Lewis.   [*Apostrophising* Rous.]   Hallo!   What's turned
him round?

Rous.   [*Speaking with intense excitement.*]   'E said fair.
"Stand by us," 'e said, "and we'll stand by you."
That's where we've been makin' our mistake this
long time past; and who's to blame for't?   [*He points
at* Roberts.]   That man there!   "No," 'e said, "fight

the robbers," 'e said, "squeeze the breath out o'
them!" But it's not the breath out o' them that's
being squeezed; it's the breath out of *us* and *ours*,
and that's the book of truth. I'm no orator, mates,
it's the flesh and blood in me that's speakin', it's the
heart o' me. [*With a menacing, yet half ashamed movement towards* ROBERTS.] He'll speak to you again,
mark my words, but don't ye listen. [*The crowd
groans.*] It's hell fire that's on that man's tongue.
[ROBERTS *is seen laughing.*] Sim 'Arness is right.
What are we without the Union—handful o' parched
leaves—a puff o' smoke. I'm no orator, but I say:
Chuck it up! Chuck it up! Sooner than go on
starving the women and the children.

> [*The murmurs of acquiescence almost drown the
> murmurs of dissent.*

EVANS. What's turned *you* to blacklegging?

ROUS. [*With a furious look.*] Sim 'Arness knows what
he's talkin' about. Give us power to come to terms
with London; I'm no orator, but I say—have done
wi' this black misery!

> [*He gives his muffler a twist, jerks his head back
> and jumps off the platform. The crowd
> applauds and surges forward. Amid cries
> of " That's enough !" " Up Union !" " Up
> Harness !"* ROBERTS *quietly ascends the
> platform. There is a moment of silence.*

BLACKSMITH. We don't want to hear you. Shut
it!

HENRY ROUS. Get down !

[*Amid such cries they surge towards the platform.*

EVANS. [*Fiercely.*] Let 'im speak! Roberts! Roberts !

BULGIN. [*Muttering.*] He'd better look out that I don't crack 'is skull.

> [ROBERTS *faces the crowd, probing them with his eyes till they gradually become silent. He begins speaking. One of the burgemen rises and stands.*

ROBERTS. You don't want to hear me, then ? You'll listen to Rous and to that old man, but not to me.   You'll listen to Sim Harness of the Union that's treated you *so fair ;* maybe you'll listen to those men from London ? Ah ! You groan ! What for ? You love their feet on your necks, don't you ? [*Then as* BULGIN *elbows his way towards the platform, with calm pathos.*] You'd like to break my jaw, John Bulgin. Let me speak, then do your smashing, if it gives you pleasure. [BULGIN *stands motionless and sullen.*] Am I a liar, a coward, a traitor ? If only I were, ye'd listen to me, I'm sure. [*The murmurings cease, and there is now dead silence.*] Is there a man of you here that has less to gain by striking ? Is there a man of you that had more to lose ? Is there a man of you that has given up *eight hundred* pounds since this trouble here began ? Come now, is there ? How much has Thomas given up—ten pounds or five, or what ? You listened to him, and what had he to say ? " None can pretend," he said, " that I'm not

a believer in principle—[*with biting irony*]—but when
Nature says : ' No further, 'tes going agenst Nature.' "
I tell you if a man cannot say to Nature : " Budge
me from this if ye can ! "—[*with a sort of exaltation*]
—his principles are but his belly. " Oh, but," Thomas
says, " a man can be pure and honest, just and merciful, and take off his hat to Nature ! " *I* tell you
Nature's neither pure nor honest, just nor merciful.
You chaps that live over the hill, an' go home dead
beat in the dark on a snowy night—don't ye fight
your way every inch of it ? Do ye go lyin' down an'
trustin' to the tender mercies of this merciful Nature ?
Try it and you'll soon know with what ye've got to
deal. 'Tes only by that—[*he strikes a blow with his
clenched fist*]—in Nature's face that a man can be a man.
" Give in," says Thomas, " go down on your knees ;
throw up your foolish fight, an' perhaps," he said,
" perhaps your enemy will chuck you down a crust."

JAGO. Never !

EVANS. Curse them !

THOMAS. I nefer said that.

ROBERTS. [*Bitingly.*] If ye did not say it, man, ye
meant it. An' what did ye say about Chapel ?
" Chapel's against it," ye said. " She's against it ! "
Well, if Chapel and Nature go hand in hand, it's the
first I've ever heard of it. That young man there
—[*pointing to* ROUS]—said I 'ad 'ell fire on my tongue.
If I had I would use it all to scorch and wither this
talking of surrender. Surrendering's the work of
cowards and traitors.

HENRY ROUS. [*As* GEORGE ROUS *moves forward.*] Go for him, George—don't stand his lip!

ROBERTS. [*Flinging out his finger.*] Stop there, George Rous, it's no time this to settle personal matters. [ROUS *stops.*] But there was one other spoke to you—Mr. Simon Harness. We have not much to thank Mr. Harness and the Union for. They said to us "Desert your mates, or we'll desert you." An' they did desert us.

EVANS. They did.

ROBERTS. Mr. Simon Harness is a clever man, but he has come too late. [*With intense conviction.*] For all that Mr. Simon Harness says, for all that Thomas, Rous, for all that any man present here can say— *We've won the fight!*

> [*The crowd sags nearer, looking eagerly up. With withering scorn.*]

You've felt the pinch o't in your bellies. You've forgotten what that fight 'as been; many times I have told you; I will tell you now this once again. The fight o' the country's body and blood against a blood-sucker. The fight of those that spend themselves with every blow they strike and every breath they draw, against a thing that fattens on them, and grows and grows by the law of *merciful* Nature. That thing is Capital! A thing that buys the sweat o' men's brows, and the tortures o' their brains, at its own price. *Don't I* know that? Wasn' the work o' *my* brains bought for seven hundred pounds, and hasn't one hundred thousand pounds been gained

them by that seven hundred without the stirring of
a finger. It is a thing that will take as much
and give you as little as it can. That's *Capital!*
A thing that will say—"I'm very sorry for you,
poor fellows—you have a cruel time of it, I know,"
but will not give one sixpence of its dividends to
help you have a better time. That's Capital! Tell
me, for all their talk is there one of them that will
consent to another penny on the Income Tax to help
the poor? That's Capital! A white-faced, stony-
hearted monster! Ye have got it on its knees; are
ye to give up at the last minute to save your miserable
bodies pain? When I went this morning to those
old men from London, I looked into their very
'earts. One of them was sitting there—Mr. Scantlebury, a mass of flesh nourished on us: sittin' there
for all the world like the shareholders in this Company, that sit not moving tongue nor finger, takin'
dividends—a great dumb ox that can only be roused
when its food is threatened. I looked into his eyes
and I saw *he was afraid*—afraid for himself and his
dividends, afraid for his fees, afraid of the very shareholders he stands for; and all but one of them's
afraid—like children that get into a wood at night,
and start at every rustle of the leaves. I ask you,
men—[*he pauses, holding out his hand till there is utter
silence*]—Give me a free hand to tell them : "Go
you back to London. The men have nothing for you!"
[*A murmuring.*] Give me that, an' I swear to you, within a week you shall have from London all you want.

R

Evans, Jago, and Others. A free hand ! Give
him a free hand ! Bravo—bravo !

Roberts. 'Tis not for this little moment of time
we're fighting [*the murmuring dies*] not for ourselves,
our own little bodies, and their wants, 'tis for all
those that come after throughout all time. [*With
intense sadness.*] Oh ! men—for the love o' them,
don't roll up another stone upon their heads, don't
help to blacken the sky, an' let the bitter sea in over
them. They're welcome to the worst that can happen
to me, to the worst that can happen to us all, aren't
they—aren't they ? If we can shake [*passionately*]
that white-faced monster with the bloody lips, that
has sucked the life out of ourselves, our wives and
children, since the world began. [*Dropping the note
of passion, but with the utmost weight and intensity.*] If
we have not the hearts of men to stand against it
breast to breast, and eye to eye, and force it back-
ward till it cry for mercy, it will go on sucking life ;
and we shall stay for ever what we are [*in almost a
whisper*] less than the very dogs.

>   [*An utter stillness, and* Roberts *stands rocking
>   his body slightly, with his eyes burning the
>   faces of the crowd.*

Evans and Jago. [*Suddenly.*] Roberts ! [*The shout
is taken up.*]

>   [*There is a slight movement in the crowd, and*
>   Madge *passing below the towing-path, stops
>   by the platform, looking up at* Roberts.
>   *A sudden doubting silence.*

ROBERTS. " Nature," says that old man, " give in
to Nature." *I* tell you, strike your blow in Nature's
face—an' let it do its worst !

> [*He catches sight of* MADGE, *his brows con-
> tract, he looks away.*

MADGE. [*In a low voice—close to the platform.*]
Your wife's dying !

> [ROBERTS *glares at her as if torn from some
> pinnacle of exaltation.*

ROBERTS. [*Trying to stammer on.*]   I say to you—
answer them—answer them——

> [*He is drowned by the murmur in the crowd.*

THOMAS. [*Stepping forward.*]   Ton't you hear her,
then ?

ROBERTS. What is it ?   [*A dead silence.*

THOMAS. Your wife, man !

> [ROBERTS *hesitates, then with a gesture, he
> leaps down, and goes away below the towing-
> path, the men making way for him.   The
> standing bargeman opens and prepares to
> light a lantern.   Daylight is fast failing.*

MADGE. He needn't have hurried !   Annie
Roberts is dead.   [*Then in the silence, passionately.*]
You pack of blinded hounds !   How many more
women are you going to let die ?

> [*The crowd shrinks back from her, and breaks
> up in groups, with a confused, uneasy
> movement.   MADGE goes quickly away below
> the towing-path.   There is a hush as they
> look after her.*

Lewis. There's a spitfire, for ye !

Bulgin. [*Growling.*] I'll smash 'er jaw.

Green. If I'd a-been listened to, that poor woman——

Thomas. It's a judgment on him for coing against Chapel.   I tolt him how 'twould be !

Evans. All the more reason for sticking by 'im. [*A cheer.*] Are you goin' to desert him now 'e's down ? Are you goin' to chuck him over, now 'e's lost 'is wife ?

> [*The crowd is murmuring and cheering all at once.*

Rous. [*Stepping in front of platform.*] Lost his wife ! Aye ! Can't ye see ?   Look at home, look at your own wives !   What's to save them ?   Ye'll have the same in all your houses before long !

Lewis. Aye, aye !

Henry Rous. Right ! George, right !

> [*There are murmurs of assent.*

Rous. It's not us that's blind, it's Roberts.   How long will ye put up with 'im !

Henry Rous, Bulgin, Davies. Give 'im the chuck !

> [*The cry is taken up.*

Evans. [*Fiercely.*] Kick a man that's down ? Down ?

Henry Rous. Stop his jaw there !

> [Evans *throws up his arm at a threat from* Bulgin. *The bargeman, who has lighted the lantern, holds it high above his head.*

Rous. [*Springing on to the platform.*] What brought

him down then, but 'is own black obstinacy? Are ye
goin' to follow a man that can't see better than that
where he's goin'?

EVANS. He's lost 'is wife.

ROUS. An' who's fault's that but his own. 'Ave
done with 'im, I say, before he's killed your own
wives and mothers.

DAVIES. Down 'im!

HENRY ROUS. He's finished!

BROWN. We've had enough of 'im!

BLACKSMITH. Too much!

> [*The crowd takes up these cries, excepting only*
> EVANS, JAGO, *and* GREEN, *who is seen to*
> *argue mildly with the* BLACKSMITH.

ROUS. [*Above the hubbub.*] We'll make terms with
the Union, lads.   [*Cheers.*

EVANS. [*Fiercely.*] Ye blacklegs!

BULGIN. [*Savagely—squaring up to him.*] Who are ye
callin' blacklegs, Rat?

> [EVANS *throws up his fists, parries the blow, and*
> *returns it.   They fight.   The bargemen are*
> *seen holding up the lantern and enjoying the*
> *sight.   Old* THOMAS *steps forward and holds*
> *out his hands.*

THOMAS. Shame on your strife!

> [*The* BLACKSMITH, BROWN, LEWIS, *and the*
> RED-HAIRED YOUTH *pull* EVANS *and* BULGIN
> *apart.   The stage is almost dark.*

The curtain falls.

ACT III

[*It is five o'clock.* *In the* Underwoods' *drawing-room,
which is artistically furnished,* Enid *is sitting on the
sofa working at a baby's frock.* Edgar, *by a little
spindle-legged table in the centre of the room, is
fingering a china-box.* His eyes are fixed on the
double doors that lead into the dining-room.

Edgar. [*Patting down the china-box, and glancing at
his watch.*] Just on five, they're all in there waiting,
except Frank. Where's he?

Enid. He's had to go down to Gasgoyne's about a
contract. Will you want him?

Edgar. He can't help us. This is a directors' job.
[*Motioning towards a single door half hidden by a
curtain.*] Father in his room?

Enid. Yes.

Edgar. I wish he'd stay there, Enid.

[Enid *looks up at him.*]

This is a beastly business, old girl?

[*He takes up the little box again and turns it
over and over.*

Enid. I went to the Roberts's this afternoon,
Ted.

Edgar. That wasn't very wise.

263

ENID. He's simply killing his wife.

EDGAR. We are you mean.

ENID. [*Suddenly.*] Roberts *ought* to give way !

EDGAR. There's a lot to be said on the men's side.

ENID. I don't feel half so sympathetic with them as I did before I went. They just set up class feeling against you. Poor Annie was looking dreadfully bad—fire going out, and nothing fit for her eat.　　　　　　　　　　[EDGAR *walks to and fro.*]
But she would stand up for Roberts. When you see all this wretchedness going on and feel you can do nothing, you have to shut your eyes to the whole thing.

EDGAR. If you can.

ENID. When I went I was all on their side, but as soon as I got there I began to feel quite different at once. People talk about sympathy with the working classes, they don't know what it means to try and put it into practice. It seems hopeless.

EDGAR. Ah ! well.

ENID. It's dreadful going on with the men in this state. I do hope the Dad will make concessions.

EDGAR. He won't. [*Gloomily.*] It's a sort of religion with him. Curse it ! I know what's coming ! He'll be voted down.

ENID. They wouldn't dare !

EDGAR. They will—they're in a funk.

ENID. [*Indignantly.*] He'd never stand it !

EDGAR. [*With a shrug.*] My dear girl, if you're beaten in a vote, you've got to stand it,

ENID. Oh ! [*She gets up in alarm.*] But would he resign ?

EDGAR. Of course! It goes to the roots of his beliefs.

ENID. But he's so *wrapped up in this company,* Ted ! There'd be nothing left for him ! It'd be dreadful !   [EDGAR *shrugs his shoulders.*] Oh, Ted, he's so old now ! You mustn't let them !

EDGAR. [*Hiding his feelings in an outburst.*] My sympathies in this strike are all on the side of the men.

ENID. He's been Chairman for more than thirty years ! He made the whole thing ! And think of the bad times they've had, it's always been he who pulled them through. Oh, Ted, you must——

EDGAR. What is it you want ? You said just now you hoped he'd make concessions. Now you want me to back him in not making them. This isn't a game, Enid !

ENID. [*Hotly.*] It isn't a game to *me* that the Dad's in danger of losing all he cares about in life. If he won't give way, and he's beaten, it'll simply break him down !

EDGAR. Didn't you say it was dreadful going on with the men in this state ?

ENID. But can't you see, Ted, Father'll never get over it ! You must stop them somehow. The others are afraid of him. If you back him up——

EDGAR. [*Putting his hand to his head.*] Against my convictions—against yours ! The moment it begins to pinch one personally——

ENID. It isn't personal, it's the Dad !

EDGAR. Your family or yourself, and over goes the show!

ENID. [*Resentfully.*] If you don't take it seriously, I do.

EDGAR. I am as fond of him as you are; that's nothing to do with it.

ENID. We can't tell about the men; it's all guess work. But we know the Dad might have a stroke any day. D'you mean to say that he isn't more to you than——

EDGAR. Of course he is.

ENID. I don't understand you then.

EDGAR. H'm!

ENID. If it were for oneself it would be different, but for our own Father! You don't seem to realise.

EDGAR. I realise perfectly.

ENID. It's your first duty to save him.

EDGAR. I wonder.

ENID. [*Imploring.*] Oh, Ted! It's the only interest he's got left; it'll be like a death-blow to him!

EDGAR. [*Restraining his emotion.*] I know.

ENID. Promise!

EDGAR. I'll do what I can.

> [*He turns to the double doors.*
> [*The curtained door is opened, and* ANTHONY *appears.* EDGAR *opens the double doors, and passes through.*
> [SCANTLEBURY'S *voice is faintly heard :* " *Past five ; we shall never get through—have to eat another dinner at that hotel !* " *The doors are shut.* ANTHONY *walks forward.*

ANTHONY. You've been seeing Roberts, I hear.

ENID. Yes.

ANTHONY. Do you know what trying to bridge such a gulf as this is like?

> [ENID *puts her work on the little table, and faces him.*]

Filling a sieve with sand!

ENID. Don't!

ANTHONY. You think with your gloved hands you can cure the trouble of the century.   [*He passes on.*

ENID. Father! [ANTHONY *stops at the double doors.*] I'm only thinking of you!

ANTHONY. [*More softly.*] I can take care of myself, my dear.

ENID. Have you thought what'll happen if you're beaten—[*she points*]—in there?

ANTHONY. I don't mean to be.

ENID. Oh! Father, don't give them a chance. You're not well; need you go to the meeting at all?

ANTHONY. [*With a grim smile.*] Cut and run?

ENID. But they'll out-vote you!

ANTHONY. [*Putting his hand on the doors.*] We shall see!

ENID. I beg you Dad!

> [ANTHONY *looks at her softly.*]

Won't you?

> [ANTHONY *shakes his head. He opens the doors. A buzz of voices comes in.*

SCANTLEBURY. Can one get dinner on that 6.30 train up?

TENCH. No, sir, I believe not, sir.

WILDER. Well, I shall speak out; I've had enough of this.

EDGAR. [*Sharply.*] What?

> [*It ceases instantly.* ANTHONY *passes through, closing the doors behind him.* ENID *springs to them with a gesture of dismay. She puts her hand on the knob, and begins turning it; then goes to the fireplace, and taps her foot on the fender. Suddenly she rings the bell.* FROST *comes in by the door that leads into the hall.*

FROST. Yes, M'm?

ENID. When the men come, Frost, please show them in here; the hall's cold.

FROST. I could put them in the pantry, M'm.

ENID. No. I don't want to—to offend them; they're so touchy.

FROST. Yes, M'm. [*Pause.*] Excuse me, Mr. Anthony's 'ad nothing to eat all day.

ENID. I know, Frost.

FROST. Nothin' but two whiskies and sodas, M'm.

ENID. Oh! you oughtn't to have let him have those.

FROST. [*Gravely.*] Mr. Anthony is a little difficult, M'm. It's not as if he were a younger man, an' knew what was good for 'im; he will have his own way.

ENID. I suppose we all want that.

FROST. Yes, M'm. [*Quietly.*] Excuse me speakin'

about the strike. I'm sure if the other gentlemen
were to give up to Mr. Anthony, and quietly let the
men 'ave what they want, afterwards, that'd be the
best way. I find that very useful with him at times,
M'm.   [ENID *shakes her head.*
If he's crossed, it makes him violent [*with an air
of discovery*], and I've noticed in my own case,
when I'm violent I'm always sorry for it afterwards.

ENID. [*With a smile.*] Are *you* ever violent, Frost?

FROST. Yes, M'm; oh! sometimes very violent.

ENID. I've never seen you.

FROST. [*Impersonally.*] No, M'm; that is so.

[ENID *fidgets towards the door's back.*]
[*With feeling.*] Bein' with Mr. Anthony, as you know,
M'm, ever since I was fifteen, it worries me to see him
crossed like this at his age. I've taken the liberty to
speak to Mr. Wenklin [*dropping his voice*]—seems to
be the most sensible of the gentlemen—but 'e said
to me: " That's all very well, Frost, but this strike's
a very serious thing," 'e said. " Serious for all parties,
no doubt," I said, "but yumour 'im, sir," I said,
" yumour 'im. It's like this, if a man comes to a
stone wall, 'e doesn't drive 'is 'ead against it, 'e gets
over it." "Yes," 'e said, " you'd better tell your
master that." [FROST *looks at his nails.*] That's
where it is, M'm. I said to Mr. Anthony this morning: " Is it worth it, sir?" " Damn it," he said to
me, " Frost! Mind your own business, or take a
month's notice!" Beg pardon, M'm, for using such
a word.

ENID. [*Moving to the double doors, and listening.*] Do you know that man Roberts, Frost?

FROST. Yes, M'm; that's to say, not to speak to. But to *look* at 'im you can tell what *he's* like.

ENID. [*Stopping.*] Yes?

FROST. He's not one of these 'ere ordinary 'armless Socialists. 'E's violent; got a fire inside 'im. What I call "personal." A man may 'ave what opinion 'e likes, so long as 'e's not personal; when 'e's that 'e's *not* safe.

ENID. I think that's what my Father feels about Roberts.

FROST. No doubt, M'm, Mr. Anthony has a feeling against him.

> [ENID *glances at him sharply, but finding him in perfect earnest, stands biting her lips, and looking at the double doors.*]

It's a regular right down struggle between the two. I've no patience with this Roberts, from what I 'ear he's just an ordinary workin' man like the rest of 'em. If he did invent a thing he's no worse off than 'undreds of others. My brother invented a new kind o' dumb waiter—nobody gave *him* anything for it, an' there it is, bein' used all over the place.

> [ENID *moves closer to the double doors.*]

There's a kind o' man that never forgives the world, because 'e wasn't born a gentleman. What I say is —no man that's a gentleman looks down on another man because 'e 'appens to be a class or two above 'im, no more than if 'e 'appens to be a class or two below.

ENID. [*With slight impatience.*] Yes, I know, Frost, of course. Will you please go in and ask if they'll have some tea; say I sent you.

FROST. Yes, M'm.

> [*He opens the doors gently and goes in. There is a momentary sound of earnest, rather angry talk.*

WILDER. I don't agree with you.

WANKLIN. We've had this over a dozen times.

EDGAR. [*Impatiently.*] Well, what's the proposition?

SCANTLE. Yes, what does your Father say? Tea? Not for me, not for me!

WANKLIN. What I understand the Chairman to say is this——

> [FROST *re-enters closing the door behind him.*

ENID. [*Moving from the door.*] Won't they have any tea, Frost?

> [*She goes to the little table, and remains motionless, looking at the baby's frock.*
>
> [*A parlourmaid enters from the hall.*

PARLOURMAID. A Miss Thomas, M'm.

ENID. [*Raising her head.*] Thomas? What Miss Thomas—d'you mean a——?

PARLOURMAID. Yes, M'm.

ENID. [*Blankly.*] Oh! Where is she?

PARLOURMAID. In the porch.

ENID. I don't want—— [*She hesitates.*]

FROST. Shall I dispose of her, M'm

ENID. I'll come out.   No, show her in here, Ellen.

[*The* PARLOURMAID *and* FROST *go out.* ENID
*pursing her lips, sits at the little table,
taking up the baby's frock. The* PARLOUR-
MAID *ushers in* MADGE THOMAS *and goes
out ;* MADGE *stands by the door.*

ENID. Come in.   What is it.   What have you
come for, please ?

MADGE. Brought a message from Mrs. Roberts.

ENID. A message ?   Yes.

MADGE. She asks you to look after her Mother.

ENID. I don't understand.

MADGE. [*Sullenly.*] That's the message.

ENID. But—what—why ?

MADGE. Annie Roberts is dead.   [*There is a silence.*

ENID. [*Horrified.*] But it's only a little more than
an hour since I saw her.

MADGE. Of cold and hunger.

ENID. [*Rising.*] Oh ! that's not true ! the poor
thing's heart—— What makes you look at me like
that ?   I tried to help her.

MADGE. [*With suppressed savagery.*] I thought you'd
like to know.

ENID. [*Passionately.*] It's so unjust !   Can't you see
that I want to help you all ?

MADGE. I never harmed any one that hadn't
harmed me first.

ENID. [*Coldly.*] What harm have I done you ?
Why do you speak to me like that ?

MADGE. [*With the bitterest intensity.*] You come out

of your comfort to spy on us ! A week of hunger, that's what *you* want !

ENID. [*Standing her ground.*] Don't talk nonsense !

MADGE. I saw her die ; her hands were blue with the cold.

ENID. [*With a movement of grief.*] Oh ! why wouldn't she let me help her ? It's such senseless pride !

MADGE. Pride's better than nothing to keep your body warm.

ENID. [*Passionately.*] I won't talk to you ! How can you tell what I feel ? It's not my fault that I was born better off than you.

MADGE. We don't want your money.

ENID. You don't understand, and you don't want to ; please to go away !

MADGE. [*Balefully*] You've killed her, for all your soft words, you and your father——

ENID. [*With rage and emotion.*] That's wicked ! My father is suffering himself through this wretched strike.

MADGE. [*With sombre triumph.*] Then tell him Mrs. Roberts is dead ! That'll make him better.

ENID. Go away !

MADGE. When a person hurts us we get it back on them.

> [*She makes a sudden and swift movement towards* ENID, *fixing her eyes on the child's frock lying across the little table.* ENID *snatches the frock up, as though it were the child itself. They stand a yard apart, crossing glances.*

S

MADGE. [*Pointing to the frock with a little smile.*]
Ah! You felt *that!* Lucky it's her mother—
not her children—you've to look after, isn't it. *She*
won't trouble you long!

ENID. Go away!

MADGE. I've given you the message.

> [*She turns and goes out into the hall. ENID,
> motionless till she has gone, sinks down at the
> table, bending her head over the frock, which
> she is still clutching to her. The double
> doors are opened, and ANTHONY comes slowly
> in; he passes his daughter, and lowers
> himself into an arm-chair. He is very
> flushed.*

ENID. [*hiding her emotion—anxiously.*] What is it,
Dad? [ANTHONY *makes a gesture, but does not speak.*]
Who was it?

> [ANTHONY *does not answer.* ENID *going to the
> double doors meets* EDGAR *coming in. They
> speak together in low tones.*]

What is it, Ted?

EDGAR. That fellow Wilder! Taken to per-
sonalities! He was downright insulting.

ENID. What did he *say*?

EDGAR. Said, Father was too old and feeble to
know what he was doing! The Dad's worth six of
him!

ENID. Of course he is.   [*They look at* ANTHONY.
> [*The doors open wider,* WANKLIN *appears with*
> SCANTLEBURY.

SCANTLEBURY. [*sotto voce.*] I don't like the look of this !

WANKLIN. [*Going forward.*] Come, Chairman ! Wilder sends you his apologies. A man can't do more. [WILDER, *followed by* TENCH, *comes in, and goes to* ANTHONY.

WILDER. [*Glumly.*] I withdraw my words, sir. I'm sorry.   [ANTHONY *nods to him.*

ENID. You haven't come to a decision, Mr. Wanklin ?   [WANKLIN *shakes his head.*

WANKLIN. We're all here, Chairman ; what do you say ? Shall we get on with the business, or shall we go back to the other room ?

SCANTLEBURY. Yes, yes ; let's get on. We must settle something.

> [*He turns from a small chair, and settles himself suddenly in the largest chair, with a sigh of comfort.*

> [WILDER *and* WANKLIN *also sit ; and* TENCH, *drawing up a straight-backed chair close to his Chairman, sits on the edge of it with the minute-book and a stylographic pen.*

ENID. [*Whispering.*] I want to speak to you a minute, Ted.

> [*They go out through the double doors.*

WANKLIN. Really, Chairman, it's no use soothing ourselves with a sense of false security. If this strike's not brought to an end before the General Meeting, the shareholders will certainly haul us over the coals.

SCANTLEBURY. [*Stirring.*] What—what's that?

WANKLIN. I know it for a fact.

ANTHONY. Let them!

WILDER. And get turned out?

WANKLIN. [*To* ANTHONY.] I don't mind martyrdom for a policy in which I believe, but I object to being burnt for some one else's principles.

SCANTLEBURY. Very reasonable—you must see that, Chairman.

ANTHONY. We owe it to other employers to stand firm.

WANKLIN. There's a limit to that.

ANTHONY. You were all full of fight at the start.

SCANTLEBURY. [*With a sort of groan.*] We thought the men would give in, but they—haven't!

ANTHONY. They will!

WILDER. [*Rising and pacing up and down.*] I can't have my reputation as a man of business destroyed for the satisfaction of starving the men out. [*Almost in tears.*] I can't have it! How can we meet the shareholders with things in the state they are?

SCANTLEBURY. Hear, hear—hear, hear!

WILDER. [*Lashing himself.*] If any one expects me to say to them I've lost you fifty thousand pounds and sooner than put my pride in my pocket I'll lose you another. [*Glancing at* ANTHONY.] It's—it's un-natural! *I don't want to* go against you, sir——

WANKLIN. [*Persuasively.*] Come, Chairman, we're *not* free agents. We're part of a machine. Our only business is to see the Company earns as much profit as it safely can. If you blame me for want of principle : I say that we're Trustees. Reason tells us we shall never get back in the saving of wages what we shall lose if we continue this struggle—really, Chairman, we *must* bring it to an end, on the best terms we can make.

ANTHONY. No!

> [*There is a pause of general dismay.*

WILDER. It's a deadlock then. [*Letting his hands drop with a sort of despair.*] Now I shall never get off to Spain!

WANKLIN. [*Retaining a trace of irony.*] You hear the consequences of your victory, Chairman?

WILDER. [*With a burst of feeling.*] My wife's *ill!*

SCANTLEBURY. Dear, dear! You don't say so!

WILDER. If I don't get her out of this cold, I won't answer for the consequences.

> [*Through the double doors* EDGAR *comes in looking very grave.*

EDGAR. [*To his Father.*] Have you heard this, sir? Mrs. Roberts is dead!

> [*Every one stares at him, as if trying to gauge the importance of this news.*]

Enid saw her this afternoon, she had no coals, or food, or anything. It's enough!

> [*There is a silence, every one avoiding the other's eyes, except* ANTHONY, *who stares hard at his son.*

SCANTLEBURY. You don't suggest that we could have helped the poor thing?

WILDER. [*Flustered.*] The woman was in bad health. Nobody can say there's any responsibility on us. At least—not on me.

EDGAR. [*Hotly.*] I say that we *are* responsible.

ANTHONY. War is war!

EDGAR. Not on women!

WANKLIN. It not infrequently happens that women are the greatest sufferers.

EDGAR. If we knew that, all the more responsibility rests on us.

ANTHONY. This is no matter for amateurs.

EDGAR. Call me what you like, sir. It's sickened me. We had no right to carry things to such a length.

WILDER. I don't like this business a bit—that Radical rag will twist it to their own ends; see if they don't! They'll get up some cock and bull story about the poor woman's dying from starvation. I wash my hands of it.

EDGAR. You can't. None of us can.

SCANTLEBURY. [*Striking his fist on the arm of his chair.*] But I protest against this——

EDGAR. Protest as you like, Mr. Scantlebury, it won't alter facts.

ANTHONY. That's enough.

EDGAR. [*Facing him angrily.*] No, sir. I tell you exactly what I think. If we pretend the men are not suffering, it's humbug; and if they're suffering,

we know enough of human nature to know the
women are suffering more, and as to the children—
well—it's damnable!

        [SCANTLEBURY *rises from his chair.*]
I don't say that we meant to be cruel, I don't say
anything of the sort; but I do say it's criminal to
shut our eyes to the facts. We employ these men,
and we can't get out of it. I don't care so much
about the men, but I'd sooner resign my position on
the Board than go on starving women in this
way.

       [*All except* ANTHONY *are now upon their feet,*
          ANTHONY *sits grasping the arms of his chair*
          and staring at his son.

SCANTLEBURY. I don't—I don't like the way you're
putting it, young sir.

WANKLIN. You're rather overshooting the mark.

WILDER. I should think so indeed!

EDGAR. [*Losing control.*] It's no use blinking
things? if *you* want to have the death of women on
your hands—*I* don't!

SCANTLEBURY. Now, now, young man!

WILDER. On *our* hands? Not on *mine,* I won't
have it!

EDGAR. We are five members of this Board; if we
were four against it, why did we let it drift till it
came to this? You know perfectly well why—
because we hoped we should starve the men out.
Well, all we've done is to starve one woman out!

SCANTLEBURY. [*Almost hysterically.*] I protest, I

protest! I'm a humane man—we're all humane men!

EDGAR. [*Scornfully.*] There's nothing wrong with our *humanity*. It's our imaginations, Mr. Scantlebury.

WILDER. Nonsense! My imagination's as good as yours.

EDGAR. If so, it isn't good enough.

WILDER. I foresaw this!

EDGAR. Then why didn't you put your foot down!

WILDER. Much good that would have done.

> [*He looks at* ANTHONY.

EDGAR. If you, and I, and each one of us here who say that our imaginations are so good——

SCANTLEBURY. [*Flurried.*] I never said so.

EDGAR. [*Paying no attention.*] ——had put our feet down, the thing would have been ended long ago, and this poor woman's life wouldn't have been crushed out of her like this. For all we can tell there may be a dozen other starving women.

SCANTLEBURY. For God's sake, sir, don't use that word at a—at a Board meeting; it's—it's monstrous.

EDGAR. I *will* use it, Mr. Scantlebury.

SCANTLEBURY. Then I shall not listen to you. I shall not listen! It's painful to me.

> [*He covers his ears.*

WANKLIN. None of us are opposed to a settlement, except your Father.

EDGAR. I'm certain that if the shareholders knew——

WANKLIN. I don't think you'll find their imaginations are any better than ours. Because a woman happens to have a weak heart——

EDGAR. A struggle like this finds out the weak spots in everybody. Any child knows that. If it hadn't been for this cut-throat policy, she needn't have died like this; and there wouldn't be all this misery that any one who isn't a fool can see is going on.

> [*Throughout the foregoing* ANTHONY *has eyed his son; he now moves as though to rise, but stops as* EDGAR *speaks again.*]

I don't defend the men, or myself, or anybody.

WANKLIN. You may have to ! A coroner's jury of disinterested sympathisers may say some very nasty things. We mustn't lose sight of our position.

SCANTLEBURY. [*Without uncovering his ears.*] Coroner's jury ! No, no, it's not a case for that ?

EDGAR. I've had enough of cowardice.

WANKLIN. Cowardice is an unpleasant word, Mr. Edgar Anthony. It will look very like cowardice if we suddenly concede the men's demands when a thing like this happens; we must be careful !

WILDER. Of course we must. We've no knowledge of this matter, except a rumour. The proper course is to put the whole thing into the hands of Harness to settle for us; that's natural, that's what we *should* have come to any way.

SCANTLEBURY. [*With dignity.*] Exactly! [*Turning to* EDGAR.] And as to you, young sir, I can't sufficiently express my—my distaste for the way you've treated the whole matter. You ought to withdraw! Talking of starvation, talking of cowardice! Considering what our views are! Except your own Father—we're all agreed the only policy is—is one of goodwill—it's most irregular, it's most improper, and all I can say is it's—it's given me pain——

> [*He places his hand on the centre of his scheme.*

EDGAR. [*Stubbornly.*] I withdraw nothing.

> [*He is about to say more when* SCANTLEBURY *once more covers up his ears.* TENCH *suddenly makes a demonstration with the minute-book. A sense of having been engaged in the unusual comes over all of them, and one by one they resume their seats.* EDGAR *alone remains on his feet.*

WILDER. [*With an air of trying to wipe something out.*] I pay no attention to what young Mr. Anthony has said. Coroner's Jury! The idea's preposterous. I—I move this amendment to the Chairman's Motion : That the dispute be placed at once in the hands of Mr. Simon Harness for settlement, on the lines indicated by him this morning. Any one second that?   [TENCH *writes in the book.*

WANKLIN. I do.

WILDER. Very well, then; I ask the Chairman to put it to the Board.

ANTHONY. [*With a great sigh—slowly.*] We have been made the subject of an attack. [*Looking round at* WILDER *and* SCANTLEBURY *with ironical contempt.*] I take it on *my* shoulders. I am seventy-six years old. I have been Chairman of this Company since its inception two and-thirty years ago. I have seen it pass through good and evil report. My connection with it began in the year that this young man was born.

> [EDGAR *bows his head.* ANTHONY, *gripping his chair, goes on.*]

I have had to do with "men" for fifty years; I've always stood up to them; I have never been beaten yet. I have fought the men of this Company four times, and four times I have beaten them. It has been said that I am not the man I was. [*He looks at* WILDER.] However that may be, I am man enough to stand to my guns.

> [*His voice grows stronger. The double doors are opened.* ENID *slips in, followed by* UNDERWOOD, *who restrains her.*]

The men have been treated justly, they have had fair wages, we have always been ready to listen to complaints. It has been said that times have changed; if they have, I have not changed with them. Neither will I. It has been said that masters and men are equal! Cant! There can only be one master in a house! Where two men meet the better man will rule. It has been said that Capital and Labour have the same interests. Cant! Their interests are as wide asunder as the poles. It has been said that the Board is only part of a machine. Cant! We *are* the machine; its brains and sinews; it is for us to lead and to determine what is to be done, and to do it without fear or favour. Fear of the men! Fear of the shareholders! Fear of our own shadows! Before I am like that, I hope to die.

> [*He pauses, and meeting his son's eyes, goes
> on.*]

There is only one way of treating "men"—with *the iron hand*. This half and half business, the half and half manners of this generation has brought all this upon us. Sentiment and softness, and what this young man, no doubt, would call his social policy. You can't eat cake and have it! This middle-class sentiment, or socialism, or whatever it may be, is rotten. Masters are masters, men are men! Yield one demand, and they will make it six. They are [*he smiles grimly*] like Oliver Twist, asking for more. If I were in *their* place I should be the same. But I am not in their place. Mark my words: one fine morning, when you have given way here, and given way there—you will find you have parted with the ground beneath your feet, and are deep in the bog of bankruptcy; and with you, floundering in that bog, will be the very men you have given way to. I have been accused of being a domineering tyrant, thinking only of my pride—I am thinking of the future of this country, threatened with the black waters of confusion, threatened with mob government, threatened with what I cannot see. If by any conduct of mine I help to bring this on us, I shall be ashamed to look my fellows in the face.

> [ANTHONY *stares before him, at what he cannot see, and there is perfect stillness.* FROST *comes in from the hall, and all but* ANTHONY *look round at him uneasily.*]

FROST. [*To his master.*] The men are here, sir.

> [ANTHONY *makes a gesture of dismissal.*]

Shall I bring them in, sir?

ANTHONY. Wait!

> [FROST *goes out,* ANTHONY *turns to face his son.*]

I come to the attack that has been made upon me.

> [EDGAR, *with a gesture of deprecation, remains motionless with his head a little bowed.*]

A woman has died. I am told that her blood is on my hands; I am told that on my hands is the starvation and the suffering of other women and of children.

EDGAR. I said " on *our* hands," sir.

ANTHONY. It is the same. [*His voice grows stronger and stronger, his feeling is more and more made manifest.*] I am not aware that if my adversary suffer in a fair fight not sought by me, it is *my* fault. If I fall under *his* feet—as fall I may—I shall not complain. That will be *my* look-out—and this is—his. I cannot separate, as I would, these men from their women and children. A fair fight is a fair fight! Let them learn to think before they pick a quarrel!

EDGAR. [*In a low voice.*] But is it a fair fight, Father? Look at them, and look at us! They've only this one weapon!

ANTHONY. [*Grimly.*] And you're weak - kneed enough to teach them how to use it! It seems the fashion nowadays for men to take their enemy's side. I have not learnt that art. Is it my fault that they quarrelled with their Union too?

EDGAR. There is such a thing as Mercy.

ANTHONY. And Justice comes before it.

EDGAR. What seems just to one man, sir, is injustice to another.

ANTHONY. [*With suppressed passion.*] You accuse me of injustice—of what amounts to inhumanity—of cruelty——

> [EDGAR *makes a gesture of horror—a general frightened movement.*

WANKLIN. Come, come, Chairman!

ANTHONY. [*In a grim voice.*] These are the words of my own son. They are the words of a generation that I don't understand; the words of a soft breed.

> [*A general murmur. With a violent effort* ANTHONY *recovers his control.*

EDGAR. [*Quietly.*] I said it of *myself*, too, Father.

> [*A long look is exchanged between them, and* ANTHONY *puts out his hand with a gesture as if to sweep the personalities away; then places it against his brow, swaying as though from giddiness. There is a movement towards him. He waves them back.*

ANTHONY. Before I put this amendment to the Board, I have one more word to say. [*He looks from face to face.*] If it is carried, it means that we shall fail in what we set ourselves to do. It means that we shall fail in the duty that we owe to all Capital. It means that we shall fail in the duty that we owe ourselves. It means that we shall be open to constant attack to which we as constantly shall have to yield. Be under no misapprehension—run this time, and you will never make a stand again ! You will have to fly like curs before the whips of your own men. If that is the lot you wish for, you will vote for this amendment.

> [*He looks again, from face to face, finally resting his gaze on* EDGAR ; *all sit with their eyes on the ground.* ANTHONY *makes a gesture, and* TENCH *hands him the book. He reads.*]

" Moved by Mr. Wilder, and seconded by Mr. Wanklin : ' That the men's demands be placed at once in the hands of Mr. Simon Harness for settlement on the lines indicated by him this mornning.' " [*With sudden vigour.*] Those in favour : Signify the same in the usual way !

> [*For a minute no one moves ; then hastily, just as* ANTHONY *is about to speak,* WILDER'S *hand and* WANKLIN'S *are held up, then* SCANTLEBURY'S, *and last* EDGAR'S, *who does not lift his head.*]

Contrary ?   [ANTHONY *lifts his own hand.*]

[*In a clear voice.*] The amendment is carried. I resign my position on this Board.

> [ENID *gasps, and there is dead silence.* ANTHONY *sits motionless, his head slowly drooping; suddenly he heaves as though the whole of his life had risen up within him.*]

Fifty years! You have disgraced me, gentlemen. Bring in the men!

> [*He sits motionless, staring before him. The Board draws hurriedly together, and forms a group.* TENCH *in a frightened manner speaks into the hall.* UNDERWOOD *almost forces* ENID *from the room.*]

WILDER. [*Hurriedly.*] What's to be said to them? Why isn't Harness here? Ought we to see the men before he comes? I don't——

TENCH. Will you come in, please?

> [*Enter* THOMAS, GREEN, BULGIN *and* ROUS, *who file up in a row past the little table.* TENCH *sits down and writes. All eyes are fixed on* ANTHONY, *who makes no sign.*]

WANKLIN. [*Stepping up to the little table, with nervous cordiality.*] Well, Thomas, how's it to be? What's the result of your meeting?

ROUS. Sim Harness has our answer. He'll tell you what it is. We're waiting for him. He'll speak for us.

WANKLIN. Is that so, Thomas?

THOMAS. [*Sullenly.*] Yes. Roberts will not be coming, his wife is dead.

SCANTLEBURY. Yes, yes! Poor woman! Yes! Yes!

FROST. [*Entering from the hall.*] Mr. Harness, sir!

[*As* HARNESS *enters he retires.*

[HARNESS *has a piece of paper in his hand, he bows to the Directors, nods towards the men, and takes his stand behind the little table in the very centre of the room.*

HARNESS. Good evening, gentlemen.

[TENCH, *with the paper he has been writing, joins him, they speak together in low tones.*

WILDER. We've been waiting for you, Harness. Hope we shall come to some——

FROST. [*Entering from the hall.*] Roberts!

[*He goes.*

[ROBERTS *comes hastily in, and stands staring at* ANTHONY. *His face is drawn and old.*

ROBERTS. Mr. Anthony, I am afraid I am a little late, I would have been here in time but for something that—has happened. [*To the men.*] Has anything been said?

THOMAS. No! But, man, what made ye come?

ROBERTS. Ye told us this morning, gentlemen, to go away and reconsider our position. We have reconsidered it; we are here to bring you the men's answer. [*To* ANTHONY.] Go ye back to London. We

T

have nothing for you. By no jot or tittle do we abate our demands, nor will we until the whole of those demands are yielded.

> [ANTHONY *looks at him but does not speak. There is a movement amongst the men as though they were bewildered.*

HARNESS. Roberts !

ROBERTS. [*Glancing fiercely at him, and back to* ANTHONY.] Is that clear enough for ye ? Is it short enough and to the point? Ye made a mistake to think that we would come to heel. Ye may break the body, but ye cannot break the spirit.   Get back to London, the men have nothing for ye ?

> [*Pausing uneasily he takes a step towards the unmoving* ANTHONY.

EDGAR. We're all sorry for you, Roberts, but——

ROBERTS. Keep your sorrow, young man.   Let your Father speak !

HARNESS. [*With the sheet of paper in his hand, speaking from behind the little table.*] Roberts !

ROBERTS. [*To* ANTHONY, *with passionate intensity.*] Why don't ye answer ?

HARNESS. Roberts !

ROBERTS. [*Turning sharply.*] What is it ?

HARNESS. [*Gravely.*] You're talking without the book ; things have travelled past you.

> [*He makes a sign to* TENCH, *who beckons the Directors. They quickly sign his copy of the terms.*]

Look at this, man! [*Holding up his sheet of paper.*]

' Demands conceded, *with the exception of those relating to the engineers and furnace-men.* Double wages for Saturday's overtime. Night-shifts as they are.' These terms have been agreed. The men go back to work again to-morrow. The strike is at an end.

ROBERTS. [*Reading the paper, and turning on the men. They shrink back from him, all but* ROUS, *who stands his ground. With deadly stillness.*] Ye have gone back on me? I stood by ye to the death; ye waited for *that* to throw me over!

        [*The men answer, all speaking together.*

ROUS. It's a lie!

THOMAS. Ye were past endurance, man.

GREEN. If ye'd listen to me——

BULGIN. [*Under his breath.*] Hold your jaw!

ROBERTS. Ye waited for *that !*

HARNESS. [*Taking the Directors' copy of the terms, and handing his own to* TENCH.] That's enough, men. You had better go.

        [*The men shuffle slowly, awkwardly away.*

WILDER. [*In a low, nervous voice.*] There's nothing to stay for now, I suppose. [*He follows to the door.*] I shall have a try for that train! Coming, Scantlebury?

SCANTLEBURY. [*Following with* WANKLIN.] Yes, yes; wait for me.   [*He stops as* ROBERTS *speaks.*

ROBERTS. [*To* ANTHONY.] But *ye* have not signed them terms! They can't make terms without their Chairman! Ye would never sign them terms!

        [ANTHONY *looks at him without speaking.*]

Don't tell me ye have ! for the love o' God ! [*With passionate appeal.*] I reckoned on ye !

HARNESS. [*Holding out the Director's copy of the terms.*] *The Board* has signed !

> [ROBERTS *looks dully at the signatures— dashes the paper from him, and covers up his eyes.*

SCANTLEBURY. [*Behind his hand to* TENCH.] Look after the Chairman ! He's not well ; he's not well —he had no lunch. If there's any fund started for the women and children, put me down for—for twenty pounds.

> [*He goes out into the hall, in cumbrous haste ; and* WANKLIN, *who has been staring at* ROBERTS *and* ANTHONY *with twitchings of his face, follows.* EDGAR *remains seated on the sofa, looking at the ground ;* TENCH, *returning to the bureau, writes in his minute-book.* HARNESS *stands by the little table, gravely watching* ROBERTS.

ROBERTS. Then you're no longer Chairman of this Company ! [*Breaking into half-mad laughter.*] Ah ! ha—ah, ha, ha ! They've thrown ye over—thrown over their Chairman : Ah—ha—ha ! [*With a sudden dreadful calm.*] So—they've done us both down, Mr. Anthony ?

> [ENID, *hurrying through the double doors, comes quickly to her father.*

ANTHONY. Both broken men, my friend Roberts !

HARNESS. [*Coming down and laying his hands on*

ROBERTS' *sleeve.*] For shame, Roberts! Go home quietly, man; go home!

ROBERTS. [*Tearing his arm away.*] Home? [*Shrinking together—in a whisper.*] Home!

ENID. [*Quietly to her father.*] Come away, dear! Come to your room!

> [ANTHONY *rises with an effort. He turns to* ROBERTS *who looks at him. They stand several seconds, gazing at each other fixedly;* ANTHONY *lifts his hand, as though to salute, but lets it fall. The expression of* ROBERTS' *face changes from hostility to wonder. They bend their heads in token of respect.* ANTHONY *turns, and slowly walks towards the curtained door. Suddenly he sways as though about to fall, recovers himself and is assisted out by* EDGAR *and* ENID; UNDERWOOD *follows, but stops at the door.* ROBERTS *remains motionless for several seconds, staring intently after* ANTHONY, *then goes out into the hall.*

TENCH. [*Approaching* HARNESS.] It's a great weight off my mind, Mr. Harness! But what a painful scene, Sir!   [*He wipes his brow.*]

> [HARNESS, *pale and resolute, regards with a grim half-smile the quavering* TENCH.]

It's all been so violent! What did he mean by: "Done us both down?" If he has lost his wife, poor fellow, he oughtn't to have spoken to the Chairman like that !

HARNESS. A woman dead; and the two best men both broken !

TENCH. [*Staring at him—suddenly excited.*] D'you know, Sir—these terms, they're the *very same* we drew up together, you and I, and put to both sides before the fight began ?   All this—all this—and—and what for ?

HARNESS. [*In a slow grim voice.*] That's where the fun comes in !

> [UNDERWOOD *without turning from the door*
> *makes a gesture of assent.*

> *The curtain falls.*

Printed by BALLANTYNE &c CO. LIMITED
Tavistock Street. Covent Garden, London

A154

DATE DUE

DISCARD

DEMCO 38-297